DAVID BRAIN

Insider Tips - Ultimate Glasgow Travel Guide 2024

Complete Hidden Gems & A Weekend itinerary

First published by David Brain 2024

Copyright © 2024 by David Brain

All rights reserved. No part of this publication may be reproduced, stored or transmitted in any form or by any means, electronic, mechanical, photocopying, recording, scanning, or otherwise without written permission from the publisher. It is illegal to copy this book, post it to a website, or distribute it by any other means without permission.

David Brain asserts the moral right to be identified as the author of this work.

David Brain has no responsibility for the persistence or accuracy of URLs for external or third-party Internet Websites referred to in this publication and does not guarantee that any content on such Websites is, or will remain, accurate or appropriate.

First edition

This book was professionally typeset on Reedsy. Find out more at reedsy.com

Contents

Preface	v
Intro to Glasgow	1
About Glasgow:	1
Past and Culture:	4
Geographical Highlights:	6
Preparing for Your Trip:	8
Must-Visit Landmarks	20
Kelvingrove Art Gallery and Museum:	20
Glasgow Cathedral:	22
The Barrowlands:	24
George Square:	27
The Vibrant Art and Tech Scene	31
UNESCO City of Music:	31
Tech Hubs in Glasgow:	32
Art Galleries and Exhibitions:	33
Live Music Venues:	35
Parks and Outdoor Activities	37
Glasgow Green:	37
Barshaw Park:	39
Clyde Muirshiel:	43
Walking Trails and Outdoor Tours:	46
Glasgow Cuisine	50
Traditional Glasgow Dishes:	50
Whisky Tasting Guide:	56
Best Places to Eat:	59

Dietary Tips and Advice:	61
Festivals and Events	64
Glasgow Festival Fringe:	64
Hogmanay Celebrations:	70
Commonwealth Games:	74
Other Noteworthy Events:	77
Practical Information	80
Getting Around Glasgow:	80
Weather and Best Time to Visit:	82
Safety Tips:	88
Useful Glasgow Phrases:	90
Hidden Gems	92
Hidden Gems in Glasgow:	92
Lesser-Known Historical Sites:	106
Unique Glasgow Experiences:	110
Sustainable Travel in Glasgow:	112
Bonus: Insider Tips from Locals	116
Bonus 1:	116
Bonus 2:	118
Bonus 3:	121
Bonus 4:	123

Preface

Glasgow is a fantastic and unique Scottish city that caters to a wide range of tastes based on what you enjoy doing as a visitor. I'm disappointed when people (particularly Glaswegians) say that Glasgow isn't a nice place to visit in comparison to Edinburgh. As a regular traveler, I can tell you that Glasgow is also a fantastic city to visit, with many unique features that make it an interesting tourist location. It is one of the world's best models of a Victorian city.

Kelvingrove Art Gallery and Museum Scotland. It's a striking example of Victorian architecture and one of the most famous landmarks in the city, well-known for its wide-ranging galleries and exhibits.

Victorian buildings and parks may be seen throughout the city, especially in the West End and the Queens Park/Battlefield area. Kelvingrove Park, in particular, is bordered by Glasgow University, Park Circus, and the Kelvingrove Art Gallery and Museum, which are all good examples of Victorian buildings. I haven't even mentioned the many Victorian bridges, train lines, and mansions. There would have been a lot more if the crooked Glasgow Corporation had not chosen to take the heart out of the city in the 1960s to build the Kingston Bridge and M8! There is an interesting past to be found throughout the city.

Victorian Townhouses, Glasgow

The People's Palace on Glasgow Green tells many amazing tales of how Glasgow grew from many little towns on the banks of a now-underground river, the Molendinar, to Scotland's biggest city.

Glasgow Green

There is also a transport museum since Glasgow was considered the Empire's second city for most of the first half of the twentieth century, with trains made in St. Rollox and ships built in Govan being shipped from the Clyde Docks across the British Empire. For nightlife, Glasgow offers many bars, restaurants, music places, sports grounds, and outdoor events in the summer, such as the Merchant City Festival and the West End Festival.

Glasgow has a great sense of humor about itself, and the overwhelming majority of people you will meet will be the most kind and welcoming you could experience anywhere!

As many others have noted, Glasgow's true highlight is its people and culture. The people of Glasgow are among the nicest in the United Kingdom. Glasgow's society is highly working-class and "real." Many people say that Glasgow is the most real place in Scotland, and I would agree. The people of Glasgow might be tough, but if they think you are right, they will support you to the end of the world. Glasgow has a wonderful history of sticking up for the little guy (and girl!).

Crowds in Glasgow

Glasgow has a good amount of skepticism and criticism directed at those in positions of power. It goes pretty far back! Glasgow has been a well-known center of labor and the left-wing movement since the industrial era, and it continues to have an impact on culture today! The stunning

People's Palace presents the story of the Red Clyde, a time when Glasgow was a combative, working-class city that openly resisted the government. Its history is fascinating and unique to Glasgow. During World War I, Glasgow was the site of notable rent strikes.

During the war, owners thought they could make more money by scaring women with removal and rent increases while their husbands and kids were away at war. What they didn't count on was that you never mess with the Glasgow working class. Glaswegians work in unity! Mary Barbour quickly arrived to put them in their place, and despite her arrest and sentence, she was able to freeze rent over the whole United Kingdom during the war!

A win for regular people. Glasgow is a city with so much personality and history that it's tough to describe it all in a few words! Indeed, this dynamic city is a must-see trip, mixing country charm with grandeur and offering a vivid picture of urban life that includes everything from postmodern architecture to well-maintained Victorian structures. There is a distinct difference here: austere modern buildings lie beside beautiful Victorian houses, resulting in a varied and interesting cityscape.

Glasgow's energy is mirrored in its people; passionate and feisty, they represent a city that may seem rough one minute and warmly friendly the next.

Finally, Glasgow gives an experience that is both powerful and delightful. Glasgow makes a lasting impression, whether you are fascinated by its old-world beauty or interested in its lively social fabric. So, once it is safe to travel again, plan a trip to this one-of-a-kind city and discover its obvious appeal. Whether you love it or are pushed by its energy,

Glasgow is a place you will not soon forget.

Intro to Glasgow

About Glasgow:

Glasgow is one of Europe's most lively and cosmopolitan towns. It boasts world-famous art collections, the best shopping in the UK outside of London, first-class sports and leisure facilities, a vast array of restaurants and bars, and the most lively and exciting nightlife in Scotland. The city is home to the Scottish Ballet, the Scottish Opera, and the Royal Scottish National Orchestra.

Just beyond the city itself lies some of Scotland's most spectacular scenery: old castles, lochs, glens, and miles of beautiful beaches. There are some of the best chances for walks, boating, trout fishing, and playing sports. Glasgow is also only 42 miles from Scotland's capital, Edinburgh.

Glasgow, Scotland

Glasgow, the largest city in Scotland and the third largest in the United Kingdom, is known for its rich past, lively cultural scene, and dynamic people. Glasgow, situated on the River Clyde in the country's western Lowlands, has played a significant role in Britain's history and current patchwork.

Geographical Settings

Glasgow is ideally positioned in the middle west of Scotland, making it a critical hub for trade and business. The city spans a total area of approximately 175 square kilometers (68 square miles), with a varied environment that includes urban buildings and green places. The River Clyde, a major physical feature, has been important in Glasgow's economic growth, historically supporting the shipbuilding industry that the city was once famous for.

Glasgow's terrain is mainly flat, especially in the city center and along the river, which has affected urban planning and growth tactics. To the north and east, the landscape becomes more varied and hilly, including areas such as Ruchill and Easterhouse that offer sweeping views of the city skyline. Glasgow experiences a moderate marine climate, marked by warm, wet winters and cool, wet summers. The closeness to the Atlantic Ocean moderates weather swings, although Glasgow is often mentioned as one of the rainier towns in the UK, which has shaped much of the outdoor activities and lifestyle choices of its residents.

Demographics:

Glasgow is a melting pot of countries, as evidenced by its population mix. According to the most recent census, the city's population is over 600,000, with a significant increase over the last decade. This rise is credited to both natural increases and immigration, with people from different ethnic groups making Glasgow their home. The city shows a younger demographic picture compared to other parts of Scotland, with a large share of its people between the ages of 20 and 44.

This age spread is largely due to an increase in students attending the city's universities and colleges, as well as young workers drawn by job opportunities in fields like banking, education, and health care. Cultural Diversity Glasgow's diverse variety is one of its most unique traits. The city is home to a large number of people of Indian, Pakistani, Chinese, and African descent, adding to a rich cultural mix. This variety is mirrored in the city's food scene, faith organizations, and cultural events. For instance, the yearly Glasgow Mela, which celebrates South Asian culture, draws thousands of tourists and is a testament to the city's mixed spirit.

Moreover, Glasgow's dedication to promoting cultural integration and peace can be seen in various community projects and policies aimed at helping ethnic minorities and creating a feeling of connection among all residents. Glasgow sticks out as a city of great physical and cultural importance. Its strategic position, diverse population, and rich cultural history make it an interesting subject of study and an important player in the United Kingdom's socio-economic environment. The city's ongoing development and adaptation to global change continue to shape its character and future, ensuring a lively and strong Glasgow for generations to come.

Past and Culture:

A Look into Glasgow's Rich Past and Different Cultures. Glasgow, a city that has undergone deep changes from its modest beginnings to its present standing as a cultural and economic powerhouse, offers an interesting historical story mixed with a rich tapestry of cultural diversity. This chapter discusses Glasgow's historical growth, cultural icons, and the arts, which collectively add to its unique character.

Historical Overview

The early beginnings and medieval Glasgow Glasgow's past go back to ancient times, but the city's major growth began with the Christian missionary Saint Mungo in the 6th century. He built a church at the place where the modern Glasgow Cathedral stands, around which the first villages were formed. By the 12th century, Glasgow was given a bishopic, becoming the religious center of Scotland. The founding of the University of Glasgow in 1451, one of the oldest universities in the English-speaking world, marked another milestone, promoting education and intellectual growth.

Industrial Expansion and Modernization:

The Industrial Revolution of the 18th and 19th centuries changed Glasgow dramatically, making it an industrial hub, mainly for ship-building and engineering. The city's population grew due to an increase in workers, making it one of the biggest towns in Britain by the 20th century. Glasgow's factories along the River Clyde were world-renowned, and during World Wars I and II, the city was a focus point for weapons production. Post-Industrial Transformation The mid-20th century decline of ships and heavy industry resulted in economic problems and social strife.

However, Glasgow's robust spirit triumphed, and the city remade itself as a center of culture, education, and services. Glasgow's selection as the European Capital of Culture in 1990 was a major turning point, beginning a time of rebuilding and artistic rebirth. Cultural Dynamics Glasgow's artistic heritage Glasgow has a storied artistic history, with famous people such as Charles Rennie Mackintosh whose original designs reflect Glasgow's artistic gifts to the world.

Numerous galleries and museums, including the Kelvingrove Art Gallery and Museum and the modern Riverside Museum, represent the city's rich artistic and economic past. Music and performing arts The city has a lively music scene that spans traditional and modern styles.

Glasgow is named by UNESCO as a City of Music. Venues like the Royal Concert Hall and the Barrowland Ballroom host shows from local and foreign acts. The city also boasts a vibrant theatre-theatre scene, with institutions like the Glasgow Royal Concert Hall and the Theatre Royal giving a wide range of shows, from opera to modern plays.

Festivals and community events

Glasgow's culture calendar is packed with events celebrating everything from movies and writing to food and drink. The Glasgow Film Festival and the West End Festival bring people from across the world, showing the city's lively cultural scene. Moreover, community events such as the yearly Glasgow Mela highlight the city's culture, having music, dance, and food from around the world. Glasgow's trip from a small church village to a busy city is a testament to its lively past and cultural wealth.

Today, Glasgow stands as a symbol of resilience and creativity, continually changing and growing. Its past of rejuvenation and cultural pride not only demonstrates the character of its people but also lays the groundwork for future developments in this vibrant Scottish city. Glasgow's ongoing cultural development ensures that it remains a major cultural and historical hub in Europe, loved by both residents and tourists.

Geographical Highlights:

River Clyde:

The River Clyde is probably the most important physical feature of Glasgow. Historically, the river was important to the city's economic growth during the Industrial Revolution, when Glasgow emerged as a major hub of shipbuilding and naval engineering. Today, they continue to play a vital role, acting as a central artery that connects different parts of the city, from the busy city heart to the calm surroundings of the Clyde Valley.

The Clyde Valley:

The Natural Sanctuary, moving from around Glasgow to Lanark in the south, is known for its rich grounds and scenic beauty, which strongly contrasts with Glasgow's urban growth. This area is dotted with parks, gardens, and natural spaces, providing residents and tourists alike with a peaceful break from the busy city life. The valley also supports a range of wildlife and hosts some of the region's most important natural places.

The Glasgow Hills:

To the north and west of Glasgow lie several groups of rolling hills, including the Kilpatrick Hills and Campsie Fells. These hills not only add to Glasgow's beautiful scenery but also offer numerous sporting possibilities, such as hikes, bird watching, and other outdoor activities. On clear days, the elevation offers stunning views over the city and across the Highlands, linking Glasgow's urban surroundings with the wild beauty of Scotland.

Glasgow's Green Belt:

Urban Containment and Preservation Surrounding the city is the Glasgow Green Belt, a policy and land use zoning plan aimed at reducing urban sprawl and protecting the wild environment around Glasgow. This green belt comprises farming land, woods, and open space that support the region's ecology and serves as a buffer zone between Glasgow and its surrounding towns and villages.

Geological foundations: Glasgow's bedrock and Glasgow's underlying rock have impacted the city's plans and infrastructure. The city is mainly built upon carboniferous soils, which have historically provided a rich base for the coal mining business.

Additionally, the presence of clay has been important in the growth of the brickmaking industry in certain places, further shaping Glasgow's industrial setting. Glasgow's physical traits are as different as they are important. From the River Clyde, which has shaped much of its history and growth, to the safe and lush green belts that circle the city, these traits offer a view into the past and a picture of the future. Understanding these features not only provides a better understanding of Glasgow's unique place within Scotland but also reveals the relationship between its natural environment and urban growth.

Preparing for Your Trip:

A trip to Glasgow, with its rich past, lively cultural scene, and unique physical features, offers an exciting and rewarding experience. Whether you're coming for leisure, work, or school reasons, planning is key to making the most of your stay. This chapter provides thorough information on what to prepare before you start on your trip to Glasgow, ensuring a smooth and enjoyable visit.

Travel Documentation and Legal Requirements: When making a trip to Glasgow, the main step is ensuring that all your travel paperwork is correct and up-to-date. This section will elaborate on the necessary documents and the importance of adhering to legal requirements for a hassle-free entry and stay.

Passport Validity: A current passport is necessary for foreign travel. Ensure your passport is good for at least six months beyond your planned date of exit from Glasgow. Some countries have laws requiring a passport to have two to four blank pages available for stamps upon entry and exit, so check your passport pages too.

Visas and Entry Permits: Visa requirements vary depending on your country, the reason for your visit, and the duration of your stay. Citizens from non-EU countries must check whether they need a visa to enter the UK. The Standard Visitor Visa is popular for tourists and allows a stay of up to six months. For longer trips or reasons like work or school, different cards are needed.

Applications for visas should be made well in advance of your trip date to allow for any delays in processing. Information on the necessary papers, registration forms, and process information can be found on the official UK government website. Electronic Visa Waiver (EVW) or e-visas might be offered to people of certain countries, allowing easy and faster entry.

Trip Insurance: Securing comprehensive trip insurance is critical. Your insurance should cover medical costs, as healthcare for non-residents in the UK can be expensive without proper coverage.

Additionally, protection from trip delays, interruptions, and lost or stolen bags will defend your funds against unforeseen situations. Ensure that your travel insurance offers coverage for possible COVID-19-related problems, such as trip delays or medical treatment if you catch the virus while traveling.

Some plans provide 24-hour support services, which can be useful in certain situations.

Documents on health and protection: Depending on your trip history, you might need to show proof of protection against certain diseases. While the COVID-19 vaccine isn't currently required for entry into the UK, rules can change, and it's wise to have your vaccination proof. Always check for the latest health warnings and entry rules before your trip.

Driver's licenses and international driving permits: If you plan to drive in Glasgow, check if your present driving license is legal in the UK. To properly drive a car, residents of many countries will need an International Driving Permit (IDP) along with their national driving license.

Customs Declarations: Be aware of what you can and cannot bring into the UK, including duty-free limits for drink, tobacco, and other things. If you're bringing a large sum of money or expensive things, you might need to report them upon entry. Understanding these rules can help avoid legal problems and fines.

Financial preparation: Proper financial planning is crucial for a hassle-free trip to Glasgow. This involves more than just saving enough money for the trip; it also includes planning how to access and handle your funds while abroad.

Here are detailed steps to ensure your financial plans are thorough and safe.

Inform your bank. Before going, inform your bank and credit card companies of your trip plans and location. This step helps prevent your account from being frozen due to suspected fake activity when transactions are identified from odd places. Most banks allow you to set trip alerts through their online banking systems or mobile apps. Acquire local currency. Having some local currency (British Pound Sterling, GBP) on hand upon arrival is important for paying initial costs such as transportation from the airport to your hotel, tips, or meals.

Although foreign exchange services are offered at airports, they often charge higher rates. Therefore, it's wise to switch a small amount of money before you leave or take GBP from ATMs upon landing for better exchange rates. Credit and debit cards are used. Credit and debit cards are widely accepted in Glasgow, making them convenient for most purchases.

Ensure your cards are allowed for international use and check with your bank about foreign transaction fees, which can add greatly to your costs. Some trip-specific credit cards offer perks such as no foreign transaction fees, points on travel spending, and extra travel insurance.

Consider travel cards. Prepaid travel money cards can be a safe and handy option for bringing large amounts of cash. These cards allow you to add funds and lock in exchange rates before your journey. They can be used like bank cards, and you can generally top them up online. Make sure the trip card you choose is accepted in the UK, and compare the fees for use and reloading.

Budgeting for the trip: Create a thorough budget for your trip, considering all possible expenses: lodging, food, transportation, fun, keepsakes, and emergencies.

- Apps and tools made for trip planning can help you keep track of your spending and stay within your limits.

- Always have a backup fund available in case of unplanned costs. Split your financial resources.

- To minimize the risk of losing access to all your funds at once (due to theft, loss, or a closed account), divide your money across different forms.

- Besides cash and cards, try using mobile payment systems such as Apple Pay or Google Wallet, which are also widely accepted in Glasgow.

- Secure your financial information. While moving, secure your financial information. For any purchases or when viewing your bank accounts online, use secure Wi-Fi links.

- Be careful of ATMs in quiet places, and always hide your PIN when entering.

- Keep a record of your bank's card numbers and customer service phone numbers stored separately from your wallet in case you need to block lost or stolen cards quickly.

Packing Essentials:

Packing successfully for Glasgow requires consideration of the city's uncertain weather and the variety of activities you may engage in.

Here's a full guide to help ensure you have everything you need for a comfy and fun trip.

- Weather-appropriate clothing: Glasgow is known for its changeable weather, which can change several times in a single day.

- Essential items include a waterproof jacket. A sturdy, open waterproof jacket is crucial for keeping dry. Look for one with a hood for extra protection against sudden downpours.

- Umbrella: Compact and strong, an umbrella provides extra rain protection, especially when you're visiting urban areas.

- Layered Clothing: Layering is key. Includes a mix of short and long-sleeve shirts, jackets, and a lightweight fleece jacket. This way, you can quickly change to different weather throughout the day.

- Warm Accessories: Depending on the season, pack a scarf, gloves, and hat, especially if coming from fall to spring when temps can be cooler.

- Footwear: Comfortable walking shoes are a must since visiting Glasgow often involves a lot of walking. Waterproof shoes or boots are recommended if you plan to come during the rainy months or if you're going into rural areas around the city.

- Chargers and adapters: The UK uses type G electricity plugs, so bring an adapter for any gadgets you plan to use or charge. Consider taking a multi-port USB charger if you have several devices, helping to reduce the number of cables needed.

Drugs and health supplies: Pack any prescription drugs you require, along with a copy of the prescription and a letter from your doctor describing your need for the medication, which can be useful if you are questioned by customs. It's also smart to bring a small first aid kit with basics like plasters, cleaning cream, pain medicines, and any over-the-counter drugs you routinely use.

Documents and essentials for a trip: Ensure that all trip documents are kept in an easily available yet safe part of your luggage.

Passports and visas: Travel insurance details; Hotel and travel bookings: Emergency numbers and important places; Miscellaneous Items: A few additional items will ensure your trip is easy and enjoyable.

Travel Guidebooks and Maps: While digital choices are available, a real map or guidebook can be useful when electronic devices run out of power or when data is absent.

Reusable water bottle: Stay hydrated while traveling around the city. Tap water in Glasgow is safe to drink.

Backpack or Day Bag: A comfy, safe bag is great for day trips and bringing the basics as you explore.

Travel Journal or Notebook: For those who like to record their adventures or need to jot down notes.

Accommodations and Transportation:

Planning your stay and how you will travel around Glasgow are crucial aspects of your trip planning.

Here's how to approach booking your rooms and knowing the local transportation choices to ensure a smooth and enjoyable stay.

Accommodations in Glasgow host numerous concerts and events throughout the year, so book early. Booking your accommodations early is recommended to secure the best rates and access, especially during peak seasons like summer or during big events such as the Glasgow International Comedy Festival or Celtic Connections.

Types of Accommodations:

Hotels: Glasgow offers a wide range of hotels, from luxury to budget-friendly. Hotels in the city center are ideal if you want to be close to major sights and nightlife. For quieter settings, try staying in the West End or near the Botanic Gardens. Bed and Breakfasts are a great choice if you want a homey feel. They are often found in quieter areas and offer a personal touch with the chance to connect with locals.Hostels are a great choice for budget tourists and solo hikers.

Glasgow's hostels often provide common areas, which are great for meeting other tourists. Managed flats: For longer stays or for those who prefer a more home-like setting, managed flats can offer a handy and cost-effective option. Using Online Platforms: Websites like Booking.com, Airbnb, and Hostelworld provide extensive lists with user reviews that can help you make an informed choice based on your price and tastes.

Transportation in Glasgow

Understanding the Public Transport System: Buses: Buses, which are primarily operated by First Glasgow, cover vast lines throughout the city and beyond. They are regular and relatively cheap, offering a good choice for getting to places not covered by trains.

Trains: Glasgow has two main train stations, Glasgow Central and Glasgow Queen Street. Trains connect the city center with the surrounding areas and other UK towns. The Glasgow Subway is an easy way to get around the city center and the West End. It's the third-oldest subway system in the world and runs a circle path with 15 stops.

Travel Passes: Day Tickets and Travelcards: For endless movement, consider buying a day ticket or a travel card. Options like the Subway Smartcard offer cheap prices and can be topped up as needed.

ScotRail Passes: If you plan to travel widely across Scotland by train, consider a ScotRail pass, which offers unlimited train travel for a set number of days.

Other transportation options: Taxis and ride-sharing are readily available, and services such as Uber run in the city, providing convenient but more expensive public transport options. Bicycles: Glasgow is becoming increasingly bike-friendly, with special paths and bike hire schemes such as Nextbike, which allow you to take a bike from numerous sites around the city.

Planning an Itinerary: Creating a well-thought-out plan is important to maximize your time and happiness in Glasgow.

Here's how to effectively plan your visit, from sightseeing to finding local eating and surprising gifts.

Research and prioritize: Start by naming the top sites and places you wish to visit. Glasgow is famous for its architectural wonders, such as the Glasgow Cathedral and the modern Riverside Museum. The Kelvingrove Art Gallery and Museum, as well as the Gallery of Modern Art, should not be missed by art lovers.

Local eateries and culinary delights: Glasgow's food scene is lively and diverse, running from traditional Scottish fare to foreign dishes. Research local favorites and must-try meals, such as haggis or a filling, full Scottish breakfast. Don't forget to explore the West End and Merchant City areas, known for their diverse eating choices.

Hidden Gems: Look for lesser-known sites and events that can offer a unique view of the city. The Hidden Gardens, Necropolis, and Sharmanka Kinetic Theatre offer fascinating alternatives to the standard travel routes.

Open Planning: Include open days in your schedule to handle weather changes, local events, or simply to rest. This freedom allows you to join in on any unplanned activities you discover or take a day to relax and soak up the city's atmosphere.

Health and safety: Taking the necessary health and safety steps is important for a worry-free trip.

Here are some tips to follow:

vaccines and health checks: In advance of your trip, consult a travel health center or your doctor to discuss any suggested vaccines or health measures. This is particularly important if you're going to areas with health warnings.

Tap Water and Dietary Considerations: The tap water in Glasgow is safe and of good quality, but if you have a sensitive stomach, sticking to bottled water might be better. Also, familiarize yourself with food safety standards in restaurants and bars.

First Aid and Emergency Contacts: Carry a basic first aid kit stocked with items like band-aids, antiseptics, pain medicines, and any specific drugs.

Memorize or keep a handy note of emergency numbers: in the UK, the international emergency number is 999. 7.

Cultural Preparation

Understanding Glasgow's culture and social etiquette can greatly improve your experience and exchanges with locals.

Language and Communication: While English is widely spoken, learning a few words in Scots or Scottish Gaelic can be admired by locals. Simple greetings or statements of thanks can go a long way in showing respect and interest in the culture.

Local Customs and Etiquette: Scots are known for their friendliness and kindness. When visiting bars, asking to buy a 'round' for the group can be a usual practice. Tipping is usually expected in restaurants (around 10% is common), but not in bars unless table service is offered.

Cultural Sensitivities: Be respectful of local customs and historical places. Always ask for approval before taking photos of people or private property.

Understanding and following local customs not only saves misunderstandings but also strengthens your relationship with the place and its people. Preparing carefully for your trip to Glasgow not only alleviates stress but also improves your travel experience. By taking care of the basics, such as travel papers and funds, packing properly for the weather, planning your stay, and knowing local norms, you set the stage for a memorable and enjoyable visit. Glasgow awaits with its stunning mix of history, culture, and natural beauty, ready to offer you a warm Scottish welcome.

Must-Visit Landmarks

Kelvingrove Art Gallery and Museum:

Kelvingrove Art Gallery and Museum:

MUST-VISIT LANDMARKS

Kelvingrove Art Gallery and Museum, located at Argyle Street, Glasgow, G3 8AG, Scotland, stands out as one of Scotland's top free tourist sites. For those looking to come, it is well connected by public transport with the nearest train stations—Partick, Charing Cross, and Exhibition Centre—all within a mile's distance. The closest subway stop is Kelvinhall, about half a mile away. Whene driving, there is a parking area on-site with different charges based on the length of stay, including a flat rate for overnight parking.

The museum's opening hours are Monday to Thursday and Saturday from 10:00 a.m. to 4:30 p.m., and on Fridays and Sundays from 11:00 a.m. to 4:30 p.m. Entry is free, providing a cheap educational experience for all guests. Kelvingrove is known for its vast and diverse collections, with over 8,000 items presented across 22 themed halls. These collections range from natural history, guns, and weapons to important artworks covering different groups and historical eras.

Highlights include Salvador Dali's 'Christ of St. John of the Cross', a Spitfire plane displayed in the west court, and an extensive collection of European art from the 18th and 19th centuries. For a better understanding of the exhibits, viewers can take free daily tours led by expert guides, which provide thorough views into the museum's past and its collections. These tours are highly popular, so coming early is advised to book a spot.The museum offers several eating choices, including a café located on the lower level and a coffee shop in the main hall, each offering a range of meals and beverages with options to suit specific dietary needs.

These places provide a chance to relax and enjoy the setting while thinking about the museum experience. To make the most of your visit to Kelvingrove Art Gallery and Museum, planning to spend at least half the day is recommended. Additionally, your visit to meet with one of the daily organ performances can provide a unique and educational cultural experience. These events feature a variety of musical pieces and are a unique aspect of the museum's offerings, improving the mood of this historic venue.

Glasgow Cathedral:

Glasgow Cathedral, a cornerstone of medieval Scotland, is built on the spot where St. Kentigern, or Mungo, was thought to have been buried around AD 612.

Glasgow Cathedral:

This famous site marks the beginnings of Glasgow. The cathedral, which spans from the 13th to the 15th centuries, is famously the only Scottish mainland church to have escaped the Reformation of 1560 undamaged.

Inside, tourists can enjoy elaborate stone carvings in the Blackadder Aisle and a remarkable collection of post-war stained glass windows, showing both medieval skill and modern artistic successes. This long-standing building not only displays architectural and historical layers, but it also serves as a testament to Glasgow's spiritual history.

Getting There: To reach Glasgow Cathedral, tourists can walk from George Square along North Hanover Street and turn right at Cathedral Street. Public transport choices include numerous city center buses, and the closest train stop is Glasgow High Street. For those driving, the church is reachable from the M8 freeway at stop 15, with close pay-and-display parking available.

Visiting Hours: The church is open to guests from April 1 to September 30, Monday to Saturday, 9:30 AM to 5:30 PM, and on Sundays from 1:00 PM to 5:30 PM. From October 1 to March 31, the hours shift to 10:00 a.m. to 4:00 p.m. Monday through Saturday and 1:00 p.m. to 4:00 p.m. on Sundays. The last entry is usually half an hour before closing. Please keep in mind that the church may be closed for lunch from 12:00 PM to 1:00 PM, and tourists should call ahead to check.

Cost: There is no entry charge, but gifts are welcome to help the upkeep of this unique place. Mobile audio guides are offered for a small fee, improving the experience with thorough narrations accessible via smartphones.

Top Attractions: The cathedral's building itself is a major draw, having a range of ancient architectural features and an amazing collection of stained-glass windows. The Lower Church houses the shrine of St. Mungo, the founder and patron saint of the city, giving historical and spiritual depth to visits. For a panoramic view of Glasgow, the nearby Glasgow Necropolis, a Victorian graveyard set on a hill close to the church, offers a wide vista of the skyline.

Tips for Visiting: Check the cathedral's schedule ahead of your visit, as it is a working church with regular prayer services that might limit guest entry during service times. Consider taking advantage of the free guided tours given by volunteer guides, which provide important insights into the cathedral's history and architectural importance. Since there are no public bathrooms at the church itself, plan to use facilities at nearby places like the St. Mungo Museum.

For photography lovers, remember that shooting inside the church is allowed, but without a flash to maintain the mood and purity of the site. A visit to Glasgow Cathedral offers a rich mix of history, design, and spiritual thought, making it a must-visit site for those visiting Glasgow.

The Barrowlands:

The Glasgow Barrowland Ballroom, known widely as a premier live music venue, is praised for having some of the world's top musical stars and drawing incredibly enthusiastic crowds.

Barrowland

With a capacity of 1,900, Barrowland has received a diverse group of foreign acts, covering a wide range of musical styles. Iconic performers like David Bowie have visited its stage, as have a plethora of acts from various music events, such as Celtic Connections, demonstrating the venue's flexibility and broad appeal.

Beyond shows, the Barrowland Ballroom offers a unique and flexible area perfect for holding indoor festivals, trade fairs, and other large-scale events. Its historical setting mixed with modern facilities makes it a sought-after spot for event organizers looking for a place with character and a rich musical history. This mix of classic charm and modern practicality ensures that the Barrowland remains a key hub in Glasgow's culture and social environment.

Getting There: You can reach Barrowland by different means of travel. If walking from the city center, it's a simple path from George Square, going north along the side of Queen Street Station, and then turning right along Cathedral Street until you reach the venue on Castle Street. For those using public transport, numerous bus lines pass near the hall, and the closest train stop is Glasgow High Street. Drivers can leave the M8 at junction 15 and follow signs straight to the venue, with nearby pay-and-display parking available. Barrowland Ballroom does not have set public visiting hours because it mainly works as an event space. The Doors normally open by the event plans, typically an hour before the show starts.

Cost: Entry costs vary depending on the event, with tickets available through a variety of sources, including the venue's own website and major booking sites. I suggest that you buy tickets in advance due to the success of the events.

Top Attractions: Barrowland is well-known for its excellent acoustics and sprung dance floor, which enhance the live music experience. The venue has held a vast array of performers, from rock bands to dance acts, making it a key stop in Glasgow's music scene. The interior has a retro charm that adds to the mood of each event.

Tips for Visiting:

Check the schedule. Review Barrowland's event calendar to choose a show that fits your taste. Arrive early: This is a good spot, as most events are only standing.

Transport planning: Given the central position, consider using public transport to avoid parking problems.

Dress appropriately: The setting can become quite warm with a full crowd, so dress in comfortable layers. Barrowland Ballroom not only offers a chance to see great live acts but also to soak in a piece of Glasgow's rich musical history.

Whether you're catching a well-known band or finding new talent, a night out at the Barrowland is sure to be enjoyable.

George Square:

Throughout the year, George Square stands as a vibrant hub for Glasgow's cultural festivities, providing notable events like Piping Live!—a celebration of traditional Scottish music—and the charming Glasgow Loves Christmas festival, which transforms the square with holiday lights, a Christmas market, and an ice rink. George Square has also caught the mind of directors.

George Square:

It famously served as a background in the popular television series "Outlander," where it was turned into a 1940s film set for the memorable proposal scene between Frank and Claire in the first season. The square was decked out with old cars and period outfits, with players dressed in trench coats, mixing among the real-life architectural wonders that define the place today.

George Square, the main public square in Glasgow, was named after King George III and laid out in 1781. It is not only the city's official heart—housing the Glasgow City Council—but also a cultural symbol. The square is adorned with a significant collection of statues and sculptures honoring Scottish leaders such as Robert Burns, James Watt, Sir Robert Peel, and Sir Walter Scott. These figures, etched in metal and stone, watch over the busy square, which continues to be a focal point for community involvement and historical thought in the heart of Glasgow.

Getting There: Because of its central location, George Square is easily accessible. It's close to the Queen Street train stop, making it simple to reach by public transit. For those driving, close parking is provided, though given its central position, public transport or walking are advised.

Features and Attractions: The square is famous for its collection of statues and sculptures, celebrating important people such as Sir Walter Scott, Queen Victoria, Prince Albert, Robert Burns, and James Watt, among others. It is often decorated with seasonal decorations like a large Christmas tree and an ice skating rink during the winter holidays, adding to its festive charm.

Activities and Usage: As a flexible public place, George Square hosts a range of events throughout the year, from public meetings and political protests to cultural fairs and parties. Its open area and central location make it a popular meeting place for both locals and tourists.

Tips for Visiting: Visit during an event. To see the park at its most lively, plan your visit during one of the many events or festivals it hosts throughout the year. shooting: The building setting and the figures provide great chances for shooting, especially with the City Chambers on the east side of the square. Leisure and observation: Take time to watch the detailed statues and busy city life, perhaps with a coffee from one of the nearby shops.

George Square offers tourists a slice of Glasgow's rich past set against a backdrop of modern city life, making it a must-visit for those looking to experience the heart of the city.

The Vibrant Art and Tech Scene

UNESCO City of Music:

Glasgow, recognized as a UNESCO City of Music since 2008, is known for its vast and diverse music scene that covers a range of styles, from modern and classical to Celtic and country. The city hosts over 130 music events each week, with notable places like the Barrowlands, known for their lively atmosphere, and the OVO Hydro, praised for their exceptional sound. For guests eager to explore Glasgow's music scene, the city offers numerous attractions and activities. Key places include the Glasgow Royal Concert Hall and the Riverside Museum, a famous rail museum.

Additionally, street art walks and visits to the Glasgow Necropolis provide greater cultural insights. Glasgow International Airport is easily accessible by bus and train to the city center. Accommodation choices vary from inexpensive hostels and hotels to luxury flats and hotels, suiting all tastes and budgets. For a fully engaging experience, consider timing your visit during big events like Celtic Connections or the World Pipe Band Championships. Participate in the local scene by visiting pubs and live music venues, taking advantage of the opportunity to explore the city's rich past and friendly culture. Comprehensive trip information and planning tools are provided through the town tourist office and the official VisitScotland website.

Tech Hubs in Glasgow:

Glasgow has quickly transitioned into a major tech hub, leveraging its rich industrial past to build a future based on digital innovation. Glasgow is creating a lively environment for startups and tech giants alike, with key developments such as the transformation of the Met Tower into a hub for tech and digital businesses for £30 million. This hub is meant to support university spinouts and a broad range of tech businesses, representing the city's active growth in the science and tech sectors. Another noteworthy project is "the Beyond," a facility at SkyPark in Finnieston, which came from a £2.5 million public-private partnership. Designed to be Europe's biggest Internet of Things (IoT) creation place, it aims to support up to 100 companies by the end of 2024.

This building underscores Glasgow's desire to become a star in smart technologies. The Glasgow Tech Fest also shows the city's drive to support its tech population. This event brings together tech workers to talk about key topics such as funding, growth, and business journeys, thereby creating a collaborative and open tech environment.

How to get there and make the most of the place: Glasgow International Airport is well connected to the city center, with regular train and bus services. The tech hubs are ideally situated, making them easily available via public transportation.

Top draws in the tech scene: Met Tower: An ancient building turned into a cutting-edge tech hub. SkyPark: Home to "the Beyond," offering spaces for IoT companies. Glasgow City Innovation District: A lively area supporting tech and digital companies.

Visiting tips: Attend events like the Glasgow Tech Fest to network and gain insights into the tech scene. Explore the larger cultural and creative scenes in Glasgow, as these are often linked with tech advances. Consider coming during Glasgow Tech Week for an extended taste of what the city's tech scene has to offer.

Whether you're a tech worker looking to grow your network or a guest interested in the mix of technology and urban development, Glasgow offers an engaging blend of history, creativity, and community.

Art Galleries and Exhibitions:

Kelvingrove Art Gallery and Museum is one of Glasgow's gems, known for its various collections that include everything from natural history to fine art. Situated in the beautiful West End near the tranquil Kelvin River, the museum is easily accessible by public transport and offers a wealth of exhibits that cater to diverse interests. It is open daily, usually from 10:00 a.m. to 5:00 p.m., with free entry, making it a must-visit for anyone interested in the range of culture Glasgow offers. The Gallery of Modern Art (GoMA), located in the busy Royal Exchange Square, is the center of Glasgow's modern art scene.

As Scotland's most visited art gallery, GoMA serves as a hub for the study of current topics through art. It hosts a range of local and foreign artworks and offers a thought-provoking program that includes brief shows and events alongside its regular displays. The gallery's operating hours suit guests throughout the week, making it an open choice for both early and late afternoon plans. The Burrell Collection provides a more unique experience, housed in Pollok Country Park's quiet setting.

This museum, named 'Museum of the Year' for its innovative approach to display, houses an odd mix of objects, including Chinese art, medieval items, and major works by famous European artists. It is an ideal spot for those looking to immerse themselves in history and art in a peaceful environment. For those interested in cutting-edge modern art, the Modern Institute is a key site. Known for its active involvement with the global art scene, the school offers a lively program across its sites, featuring both rising and known artists. Its shows are known for pushing standard limits and encouraging critical debate around current art issues.

Tips for visiting: Plan ahead: Check online for any special shows, events, or short bans to make the most of your stay. Allow time. Don't rush your stay. Spend time with the exhibits that interest you most, and consider returning if you want to explore more.

Guided tours: Many galleries offer guided trips, which can provide a better view of the artworks and their settings.

Interactive and familial activities: Look for classes, artist talks, and engaging guides that enhance the experience, especially if you are traveling with children.

Local amenities: Many galleries have cafes, or they are located near restaurants and cafes. Plan for breaks during your trips to relax and think about the art you've seen. These galleries not only highlight Glasgow's rich artistic history and current liveliness but also provide a welcoming atmosphere for both art fans and casual tourists.

Live Music Venues:

Glasgow's live music scene is nothing short of exciting, offering a rich mix of places that cater to all tastes. Whether you're into the raw sounds of punk rock or the emotional echoes of traditional Scottish tunes, this city has a spot for you. Let's dive into some of the city's standout places, each with its own unique vibe and musical offering. First up, Nice N Sleazy on Sauchiehall Street is a true picture of Glasgow's diverse music scene. This place is a mixing pot of styles, where one night you could catch a punk rock gig and the next, a soulful acoustic set. It's not just a music place; it's a cultural event, mixing live acts with good food and a lively atmosphere.

Then there's King Tut's Wah Wah Hut, a famous spot in the heart of the city. This place is like a rite of passage for rising acts, having held some of the big names in music before they hit the big time. The small setting here means you're not just watching a show; you're part of the scene, up close with the music that could very well be shaping tomorrow's charts.

For those who lean towards a place with character and history, The Clutha is a must-visit. Located on Stockwell Street, it's one of Glasgow's oldest clubs and a hub for nightly live music. The place has a friendly vibe, making it perfect for enjoying a variety of musical styles from local and foreign acts, complemented by a great selection of drinks. Oran Mor, set in a beautifully converted church in the West End, offers a mix of classic and creative musical acts. Its upstairs theater and the basement provide two very different atmospheres for shows, making it a flexible choice for music fans.

The beautiful paintings and the architectural grandeur add to the draw, creating a background that's as memorable as the music. Not to be ignored, the Scotia Bar is where the city's musical past and present meet. It is one of Glasgow's oldest bars and has a long history of hosting lively rock and blues nights. The Scotia is a place where you can feel the city's musical heartbeat, with shows that range from local bands to famous global artists.

Lastly, SWG3 in the West End is more than just a place; it's a culture area that hosts everything from music events to art exhibitions. This place bursts with innovation, providing a space where music and other forms of art meet, providing a complete cultural experience. Each of these places not only shows the range of Glasgow's live music choices but also represents a piece of the city's cultural fabric. They're approachable, each with its own charm and a schedule of acts that show the lively mix of Glasgow's music scene.

Whether you're a local or a tourist, these places offer amazing nights filled with good music and great vibes.

Parks and Outdoor Activities

Glasgow Green:

Glasgow Green, a green area tucked in the heart of Glasgow, is a testament to the city's commitment to public places. It is the oldest park in Glasgow and serves as a green lung for the busy city, giving residents and tourists alike a peaceful escape. The park's strategic position on the north bank of the River Clyde offers beautiful riverside walking tracks that invite relaxed strolls and reflective moments. The People's Palace, a museum dedicated to the city's social history, sits as a symbol of Glasgow's cultural heritage, giving a tale that spans the growth of the city through the eyes of people

The history and significance of Glasgow Green are rich and varied. Established in the 15th century, it is not only Glasgow's oldest park but also one of the most historically important public places in Europe. Originally used as a shared grazing ground, Glasgow Green has grown to become a central hub for the city's social and leisure activities. It has been a witness to the ebb and flow of Glasgow's history, from public killings that spoke to the darker parts of its past to the lively political protests that shaped its future. The park has been a medium for the city's growth, representing the changing wants and values of its people over time.

Main Attractions: At the heart of Glasgow Green is the People's Palace, a cultural icon that represents the spirit of the city. The museum and gallery within provide a look into the daily lives of Glaswegians, tracing the city's past through personal stories and objects. Adjacent to the People's Palace, the Winter Gardens offer a green haven of foreign plants, a testament to the city's natural interests. The Doulton Fountain, a towering structure hailed as the world's largest ceramic fountain, and Nelson's Monument, a tribute to Admiral Horatio Nelson, are other notable features that add to the park's attraction. These sights not only improve the aesthetic appeal of Glasgow Green but also serve as landmarks of the city's historical and cultural journey.

How to get there: Glasgow Green is easily accessible from the city center. Visitors can take a bus, cab, or enjoy a beautiful walk. The Line 18 bus offers a straight path, while a short cab ride will whisk you there in minutes. For those who prefer to walk, the trip is a nice stroll through Glasgow's lively streets.

Best Time to Visit: The park is a year-round site, but the best time to visit is during the summer months, when the weather is most suitable for outdoor activities. July is typically the best month, perfect for enjoying the full beauty of Glasgow Green.

Accessibility: Glasgow Green is committed to being open to all. The park has been recognized for its efforts with the Gold Level of Attitude in Everything's Charter of Best Practice, ensuring services such as accessible toilets and parking are available.

Entry Fees and Regulations: The park is open to the public 24/7, with no entry fee. Visitors are invited to appreciate the park's natural beauty and history by sticking to written laws and guidelines.

Safety Tips: While Glasgow Green is a safe setting, tourists should stay aware of their surroundings, especially during events. It's recommended to check the weather forecast, dress properly, and always keep personal items secure.

Photography Tips: For photography fans, the park offers a plethora of subjects, from the architectural beauty of the People's Palace to the natural charm of the Winter Gardens. Early morning or late afternoon light offers the best conditions for catching the park's landscapes.

Nearby activities and activities: Beyond Glasgow Green, the city is bustling with activity. Kelvingrove Park and the Scottish Football Museum offer additional cultural and leisure opportunities. The lively Merchant City, with its array of eating and buying choices, is just a short walk away. Glasgow Green is not just a park; it's a live record of Glasgow's past and present, a place where nature, culture, and history combine to offer a unique experience for all who come.

Barshaw Park:

Barshaw Park, a beloved green area in Paisley, Scotland, is a haven for those wanting peace from the urban bustle. This 55-acre park, with its vast stretches of well-manicured grass and old trees, offers a beautiful setting for a variety of outdoor activities. The park's design perfectly mixes natural beauty with leisure facilities, creating an environment that is both energizing and relaxing. Visitors are met by the lovely sight of families relaxing, fitness enthusiasts running along the walks, and children playing in the play areas. The park's closeness to the town center makes it a popular spot for locals and tourists alike, who are drawn to its peaceful vibe and the chance to bond with nature.

History and Significance:

The land that is now Barshaw Park was once part of a farm owned by the Arthur family, famous local businessmen. In a major act of charity, the family sold the land to Paisley Burgh Council in 1911, paving the way for the creation of this public park. Officially opened on June 15, 1912, Barshaw Park quickly became a center point for community life in Paisley. Over the years, it has played host to countless public events, from joyful celebrations to serious commemorations. Barshaw House, the grand house that once controlled the land, has watched the park's growth from its days as a private residence to its current form as luxury flats. This shift mirrors the larger changes in Paisley's social and economic situation over the past century.

Main sites: Barshaw Park's array of sites caters to tourists of all ages and hobbies. The boating pond, a feature of the park, is a hub of activity where one can enjoy the simple pleasure of feeding ducks or the excitement of steering a rented boat. The walled garden, a botanical gem, is a riot of colors and scents, providing a peaceful spot for reflection. For the daring, the BMX track provides an exciting rush, while the tiny railway catches the minds of children and train fans alike.

The swing park is a delight for younger guests, and the city golf course tests players with its well-designed holes. The park's calendar is filled with special events like funfair days and open gala days, which bring the community together in celebration and add to the park's lively atmosphere.

How to get there: Visitors can reach Barshaw Park via public transport with bus lines 38 and 9, or by train with the ScotRail service. For those driving, there is ample parking available around the park.

Best to visit: The park is open year-round, but the best time to visit is during the summer months when the model train runs and the full beauty of the grounds can be appreciated.

Accessibility: Barshaw Park is accessible, providing easy entry and features such as play areas with tools for special needs. The Rowantree Cafe gives food and drinks to visitors.

Entry Fees and Regulations: The park is free to enter, and tourists can enjoy many of its features at no cost. However, there may be charges for specific events, like the golf course and model railway.

Safety Tips: Children should be attended by an adult on weekends. The play park is intended for safe fun, with items suited for different ages.

Photography Tips: Capturee the beauty of Barshaw Park by focusing on its diverse settings, from the quiet fishing pond to the colorful walled garden. Early morning or late afternoon light can add a magical touch to your photos.

Nearby attractions and activities: Lagoon Leisure Centre: The Lagoon Leisure Centre is a cornerstone of community life in Paisley, offering a wide range of events for all ages. With spaces for swimming, exercise classes, and different sports events, it's a place where health and fun go hand in hand. The center boasts a modern exercise room, a free-form pleasure pool with a wave machine and slide, and a separate teaching pool for learners. It's a great spot for families looking to stay active or for people wanting a complete workout.

St. Mirin's R.C. Cathedral: St. Mirin's R.C. Cathedral stands as a symbol of faith and history in Paisley. Dedicated to the patron saint of the town, it's the mother church of the Catholic Diocese of Paisley. The cathedral's building is a mix of neo-Romanesque style with an airy arched interior, and it houses a pulpit with a picture of the Sermon on the Mount carved in relief from blond sandstone. The church is not only a place of worship but also a monument to the town's religious heritage.

Paisley Abbey: Paisley Abbey is a great trove of history, dating back to its creation in the 12th century. It has served as a village church, a Cluniac abbey, and a tourist attraction. The Abbey played a key role in Scotland's past, being thought to have taught William Wallace and being the final resting place of several Scottish lords. Today, it stands as a testament to Paisley's past, with its beautiful architecture and famous ruins drawing tourists from near and far. Paisley Town Hall is a hub of cultural activity, hosting a variety of events that cater to all tastes. From comedy shows and live music to fairs and community events, the town hall is a lively place that brings entertainment to the heart of Paisley.

With its recent improvements, the hall is set to attract more shows and events, making it a must-visit for anyone looking to experience the local arts scene.

Sma' Shot Cottages: Sma' Shot Cottages provide a unique look into the lives of the weavers who were at the heart of Paisley's cloth industry. These ancient houses, dating back to the 18th and 19th centuries, have been kept to showcase the living and working conditions of the time.

Visitors can explore the weaver's house, learn about the Sma' Shot Day party, and enjoy the tea room, where stories of the past come to life. The houses are a testament to the town's rich weaving history and are an important stop for anyone interested in Scotland's industrial past. These sites, each with their own story and importance, form a patchwork of events that show the cultural wealth of Paisley. Whether you're a history buff, an art lover, or simply looking for a day out with the family, these sites offer something for everyone. Barshaw Park is more than just a park; it's a haven where nature, history, and community come together to create a place for everyone to enjoy.

Whether you're a local or a tourist, the park's open arms invite you to explore and make memories amidst its green embrace.

Clyde Muirshiel:

Clyde Muirshiel Regional Park: A Gateway to Natural Splendor situated in the heart of Scotland, Clyde Muirshiel Regional Park is a wide painting of natural beauty, stretching over 108 square miles of the South Clyde waterway. It's a place where the land tells stories of old times, and current conservation efforts combine to create a haven for both wildlife and people.

History and Significance

The park's story began in the 1940s, a tale knitted through the fabric of Scotland's post-war age. It was in 1990 that Clyde Muirshiel was officially named, showing a resolve to protect the region's beautiful scenery, various ecosystems, and the cultural marks left by generations past. This park is not just a swath of land; it's a living library, teaching tourists about the delicate balance of nature and the importance of saving our world for future explorers.

Main attractions: The Clyde Muirshiel is a treasure trove of natural wonders.

Muirshiel Visitor Center: Step into a world of quiet forests and rolling heather moorland hills. Here, the air is filled with the calls of native birds, and the scenery offers a haven for those wanting to watch Scotland's wildlife in its most natural form.

Castle Semple Visitor Center: The Loch's waters are a mirror reflecting the sky, a playground for outdoor lovers. Cyclists and walkers find comfort and challenge on the trails that ribbon around the water, making it a hub of activity and community. 3

Greenock Cut Visitor Centre: Perched with views that stretch to the distance, this center offers a glimpse into Scotland's industrial past through the Greenock Cut canal, while providing a perfect setting for a family lunch or a quiet moment to soak in the vistas.

Clyde Muirshiel Regional Park is more than just a location; it's an event that stays with you. It's the sound of leaves underfoot, the whisper of the bay against the shore, and the sight of the mountains reaching for the sky. It's where every visit paints a new picture, and every picture tells a story of Scotland's ongoing charm. Welcome to Clyde Muirshiel, where the trip into Scotland's heart starts.

How to get there: The park is accessible by a variety of means, including a train: from Glasgow Central to Lochwinnoch station, followed by a short trip to the park. Bus: Services run from Glasgow to the park's vicinity. Car: an easy drive from Glasgow, with ample parking available at the tourist centers.

Best Time to Visit: The park is open year-round, but the best time to visit is during the summer months when the tourist centers offer longer hours and a full range of activities and events are available.

Accessibility: Clyde Muirshiel is dedicated to equality, with equipment like modified sailing dinghies, boats, and hand bikes to suit guests of all abilities.

Entry Fees and Regulations: Entry to the park is free, though charges apply for certain outdoor sports and events. The park operates with a focus on sustainability and caring for the natural environment.

Safety Tips: While visiting the park, it's important to take personal responsibility for your safety. Always carry a backup means of guidance and heed any advice given by the park rangers.

Photography Tips: For shooters, the park offers beautiful scenery and wildlife. Early morning or late afternoon light provides the best conditions for capturing the natural beauty of Clyde Muirshiel.

Castle Semple Country Park, just a short distance from Clyde Muirshiel, has its own set of charms. This park is a hub for outdoor lovers, having a range of tracks for walking, running, and riding. The pond provides a quiet setting for water sports, with choices for sailing, kayaking, and even accessible outdoor activities. Visitors can also watch wildlife or simply relax with a coffee while taking in the amazing views. Largs Sea Front: A bit further away lies the Largs Sea Front, a beautiful coastal walkway that offers amazing views of the Firth of Clyde.

It's an ideal spot for a relaxed walk, with the port at one end and the famous Nardini's Ice Cream Parlor at the other. The area is also known for its Viking history, with the Vikingar Center giving views into Scotland's Norse connections. Paisley Abbey: For those interested in history, Paisley Abbey is a must-visit. This amazing place dates back to the 12th century and has played a major role in Scottish history.

It was here that William Wallace was taught and where several members of the Stewart royal line are buried. The Abbey is a treasure trove of building beauty and historical importance, giving a glimpse into Scotland's past.These sites provide a wonderful complement to the natural beauty of Clyde Muirshiel Regional Park, giving tourists a rich mix of experiences that blend Scotland's natural glory with its cultural and historical history.

Walking Trails and Outdoor Tours:

Go on a trip through Clyde Muirshiel Regional Park, a wide stretch of natural beauty that stands as Scotland's biggest regional park. This haven for outdoor enthusiasts offers a rich patchwork of walking trails and outdoor tours, each flowing through the park's diverse landscapes to cater to travelers of every stripe. The park's famous past began in the 1940s with the Clyde Valley Plan, which envisioned the area as a cornerstone for leisure and protection. Officially coming into being in 1990, Clyde Muirshiel has since evolved into a crucial green space, a refuge for wildlife, and a lush escape that has touched the lives of millions.

Clyde Muirshiel's draw is its natural beauty. The park is a mix of environments, from quiet forests to rolling heather grassland hills. It welcomes adventure and discovery, whether it's climbing the volcanic heights of Windy Hill, tracing the historic outlines of the Greenock Cut, or discovering the past at the dormant Barytes mine. The park also serves as a refuge for rare wildlife, including the elusive hen harrier, giving tourists a chance to watch these beautiful birds in their natural setting.

Trail Experiences: The park's trails offer a range of experiences, from calm walks that pass through soft landscapes to difficult hikes that ascend to the park's highest points. Each walk is a call to interact with the park's rich variety, to watch the balance of plants and wildlife, and to feel the pulse of the natural world.

Outdoor Adventures: Beyond the tracks, Clyde Muirshiel's outdoor trips provide a greater experience of the park's wonders. These led experiences range from educational nature walks to exciting outdoor activities, all meant to promote a link with the environment and reveal the secret gems of the park's vast wildness.

A live landscape: Clyde Muirshiel is more than a park; it's a live landscape that changes with the seasons. It's a place where protection and pleasure go hand in hand, where the history of the land is respected, and where every tourist can find their own way to discovery. Clyde Muirshiel Regional Park is a testament to the lasting beauty of Scotland's natural heritage. It's a place where history is living, where excitement awaits, and where the spirit of the woods is available to all. So come and walk its roads, breathe its air, and leave with experiences that will last a lifetime.

How to Get There: The park is accessible by various modes of transportation. You can take a train from Glasgow Central to Lochwinnoch or drive to the park, which is located near Lochwinnoch, Renfrewshire. For those choosing public travel, buses run daily from nearby cities. Clyde Muirshiel welcomes guests year-round, but the best time to visit is during the summer months, when the Visitor Center is open and the trails are most accessible. The park's tracks and walks are open daily, ensuring that every visit is filled with new discoveries. Accessibility: The park prides itself on being available to all. With features like modified Hansa sailing dinghies, kayaks, and wheely boats, everyone can enjoy the bay.

Additionally, there are modified hand bikes and trikes available for land activities. Entry Fees and Regulations: Entry to Clyde Muirshiel is free, although certain outdoor sports and Countryside Ranger events incur charges. The park runs with a commitment to protection, so guests are urged to respect the natural surroundings and stick to the Scottish Outdoor Access Code.

Safety Tips: When visiting the park, it's important to be prepared. Carry a backup means of guidance, dress properly for the weather, and stay aware of your surroundings. The park's team is always ready to help with any questions or concerns. Photography Tips: For photography fans, Clyde Muirshiel is a dream. For the perfect shot, capture the amazing scenery during the golden hour.

Remember to respect wildlife and use proper lenses to capture animals without disturbing them.

Nearby Attractions and Activities: Beyond the park, there's much to enjoy. Visit the famous Castle Semple Country Park, engage in water sports at Castle Semple Loch, or take a short trip to the sandy Lunderston Bay. For history buffs, the Collegiate Church and Castle Semple offer a glimpse into the past. Clyde Muirshiel Regional Park is more than just a walking spot; it's an experience that connects you with nature and history. Whether you want peace or excitement, this park has something for everyone. So lace up your boots, pack your camera, and get ready to enjoy the great woods!

Glasgow Cuisine

Traditional Glasgow Dishes:

When it comes to food, Glasgow doesn't have the best image. After all, the city has the unfortunate reputation of being one of the most risky in the United Kingdom. However, while the traditional Scottish breakfast and the many deep-fried treats from the ubiquitous chip shops in Glasgow city center aren't exactly the best thing for you, that doesn't mean they aren't delicious food.

Furthermore, Scottish cuisine is more than just fried food. Drop off your bags at a Bounce luggage storage in Glasgow, and you can dive into Scottish food and be surprised by what you find. Glasgow has come a long way in recent years, and you're likely to find great Indian meals, French food, and Asian fusion food as well as Scottish classics like haggis.

Plus, the city offers everything from a fancy eating experience to the best street food in Glasgow, so there are choices to fit every budget. And thanks to Glasgow's best veggie restaurants, it's not hard to enjoy Scottish food even if you don't eat meat.

Scottish Breakfast: The Scottish breakfast is a heart attack on a plate, but it's also one of the most delicious things you'll ever eat. And there's no better place to enjoy one than Cafe Wander's peaceful environment. This popular Glasgow breakfast spot serves up some of the best egg dishes in town, as well as delicious sausage, beans, and black pudding (a type of blood sausage). The amounts are big, so make sure you come here with a large stomach.

A classic Scottish breakfast is close to an English one, but there are some minor changes. Expect fried eggs (or possibly scrambled eggs), tattie scones (a kind of potato cake), fried mushrooms, grilled tomatoes, baked beans, bacon, sausage, buttered toast, and black pudding. This enormous meal means you can easily skip lunch and maybe dinner as well, but it is an excellent hangover cure as well as a famous item of Scottish food.

A deep-fried Mars bar is exactly what it sounds like: a chocolate bar that has been dipped in batter and cooked. It might not be the best snack in the world, but it's definitely one of the most delicious, and you can find it at many of the chip shops in the city center. The deep-fried Mars bar began in Scotland, and while it's not clear exactly where or when, there are many ideas.

One common story is that it was made by a chip shop owner in 1995 who was looking for a way to use up some extra batter. Another idea is that it was Aberdeenshire in the 1980s. Either way, this Scottish food has become something of a global craze, and you can now find deep-fried chocolate bars everywhere.

Haggis is a traditional part of Scottish food made from sheep's heart, liver, and lungs that are chopped and mixed with flour, onions, and spices, then put into a sheep's stomach and slow-cooked. It might not sound tasty, but it's delicious, and you can find it in many places in Glasgow.

Haggis is a popular food in Scotland, and there are many different ways to eat it. You can eYou can enjoy it as part of a traditional Scottish breakfast, or you can have it with neeps (turnips) and tatties (potatoes) for lunch or dinner. You can also buy haggis ready-made from many stores in Glasgow or even order them online. You'll also find that haggis has changed with the times. This traditional dish can be very varied, so expect to find versions like deer haggis and even haggis pakoras on the plates of place Bru, a bright orange fizzy soft drink, is incredibly popular in Scotland.

In fact, it's so famous that it's often referred to as Scotland's other national drink (after whisky, of course). Irn Bru has been made in Scotland since 1901, and its unique taste is created by 32 different natural spices. It's also said to be an effective hangover cure, which might explain its appeal. Irn Bru is pretty much everywhere in Glasgow, from stores to small shops, and you can even buy it online. If you're not a fan of the taste, then you can always buy Irn Bru-flavored sweets or ice cream instead.

Tablett is a Scottish sweet made from sugar, condensed milk, and butter that is boiled until it has a thick, creamy consistency. It's then left to set, where it is best described as similar to fudge. Like fudge, it can sometimes come with nuts, but at its most basic, it is simply flavored with vanilla. Don't go too crazy on this one. The high sugar level will cause havoc on both your teeth and your stomach!

Smoked Haddock: Smoked Haddock is a Scottish treat that is often served for breakfast, lunch, or dinner. It's made by cooking fresh haddock over a wood fire, which gives it a unique taste. Smoked haddock can be found in many of Glasgow's fish and chip shops, as well as in some stores and restaurants. It's generally served with chips (French fries), peas, and fish sauce.

And if you're looking for one of Glasgow's best fish restaurants, head to The Buttery at Two Fat Ladies. Afternoon tea is a truly British custom, and Glasgow is no exception. This light meal or snack consists of sandwiches, cakes, and sweets, as well as a pot of tea. You can find afternoon tea being served in many of the hotels and bars in Glasgow city center. If you want to go somewhere special, then you can book a table at one of the city's afternoon tea places, such as The Willow Tea Place or Cupcake Coffee Company.

It makes for a very polite way to beat an afternoon hunger and enjoy a classic part of British culture, along with some delicious food but Windows Restaurant and the Carlton George Hotel offer afternoon tea with a view from their rooftop restaurants in Glasgow. Porridge is a classic Scottish dish made from oats that are boiled in water or milk. It's generally eaten with sugar or fruit, and it's a favorite breakfast food. While oats might not be the most exciting food on this list, they're definitely worth trying if you're in Scotland.

You can find it being served in many bars and restaurants in Glasgow, or you can make it yourself at home using Scottish oats.

Cullen Skink is a classic Scottish soup made from smoked haddock, potatoes, and onions. It's thick, creamy, and delicious; it's a favorite starter or main dish in Glasgow. Traditionally, this famous Scottish food is made with finnan haddie, which is a local fish caught in the seas off Glasgow. However, any smoked haddock will do. You can find cullen skink on the lists of many places in Glasgow, or you can buy it ready-made from stores. If you want to try making it yourself, then there are plenty of recipes available online.

Macaroni Pie and Chips: This may not appear to be the most well-known Scottish food item on the menu, but in recent years, it has won its place alongside Scottish classics like haggis. Macaroni pie is a meal made from macaroni pasta, cheese, and a creamy sauce, all baked in a pastry crust.In Glasgow, it's often eaten with chips (French fries) as a main course. You can find it being served in many fish and chip shops, as well as some stores. If you're trying to stick to a low-carb diet, this isn't the way to do it. Nor is it exactly a fine eating experience.

However, it is an excellent way to indulge in the old tradition of Scotch pie, and it will certainly keep you filled up to explore the city. Pair it with a local craft drink, and you've got a great meal.

Black pudding is a traditional part of the famous Scottish breakfast, but it is special enough to get its place on this list. This blood sausage is made from pork, beef, or lamb, and it's a must-try for anyone with a sense of excitement.You can find black pudding being served in many of the breakfast bars and restaurants in Glasgow. It's generally made with eggs, bacon, sausage, tomatoes, and mushrooms. If you're not used to eating blood sausage, then it might take a little getting used to.

But it's worth trying if you're in Scotland and looking to taste unique flavors. Cranachan is a classic Scottish treat made from whipped cream, whisky, oatmeal, and fresh raspberries. It's rich, creamy, and tasty; it's the perfect way to round off a meal. Cranachan is generally made with local products, so you'll be able to taste the very best of Scottish food.

If you're not a fan of whisky, then don't worry; there are plenty of non-alcoholic forms of this dessert available too.

Curry: What makes something a traditional dish? How long does it take for a type of food to be adopted into the society of a nation? These are questions you may find yourself wondering over a delicious butter chicken or vindaloo when you pop into any of the thousands of curry places you'll find in Glasgow. Curry, of course, has its roots in Indian cuisine. But with mass immigration to the UK from India following the Second World War, curry soon became a famous dish in Britain, including Scotland.

Now, curry is as much a part of Scottish cooking as haggis and hot food. You can find curry being served in restaurants and bars all over Glasgow. There's a huge range of different soups to choose from, so you're sure to find one that suits your taste. Curry places in Glasgow run the gamut from high-end to cheap basements, so you can find something to suit any mood. Some of our favorites include Mother India's Cafe, Dakhin, and Obsessions of India.

Scottish salmon is world-renowned for its quality, and it's one of the most famous Scottish foods. The rich, fatty meat of this fish is absolutely wonderful, and it can be cooked in several ways. You can find Scottish salmon being served in places all over Glasgow. It's usually smoked, fried, or baked, and it's often eaten with potatoes and veggies.

If you're looking for a healthy option, then cooked salmon is a good pick. But if you're in the mood for something a little richer, then smoked salmon will hit the spot. Glasgow is a great place to try Scotland's classic foods. You'll find everything you could possibly want to eat in this city, from a luxurious fine dining experience to delicious street food, from haggis and potatoes to Scotch pies, delicious stews, and fusion food.

Of course, many classic Scottish foods aren't the best things in the world. That's okay when you're on holiday, but if you're afraid of going home with some extra pounds, don't be. Try out some of the best climbing trails in Glasgow to burn off those extra calories and earn the feast you'll be having in the city. The best food in Glasgow is just waiting to be found.

Hunt down some of these great traditional meals, and you'll be soaking yourself in the history and culture of Scotland while you explore Glasgow. There are few better ways to learn about the country than through its food, so save room for these classics of Scottish cooking, and you'll have an incredibly delicious holiday.

Whisky Tasting Guide:

Savoring the Spirit of Scotland (Continued) As we dig deeper into the heart of Scottish whisky, let's expand our knowledge and respect for this liquid gold. The whisky journey is as complex as its tastes, and knowing its details is key to becoming a true fan.

The Essence of Scottish Whisky: How is Scotch whisky made? The process starts with malting, where barley is soaked in water and allowed to sprout. It's then dried in a kiln, often over peat, which gives it a smoky taste. The malt is ground into flour, mixed with water, and boiled to trigger enzymes that turn carbs into sugars. This mash' is then fermented with yeast, making a beer-like liquid called 'wash.' The wash is distilled twice in copper pot stills, focusing on the alcohol and tastes.

Finally, it's stored in wood boxes, building its flavor over time. What do 'Single Malt' and 'Single Grain' mean? 'Single Malt' refers to whiskey made from only dried barley, water, and yeast at a single distillery. 'Single Grain,' however, can include other grains and is also made at a single brewery. Both can offer a range of tastes, from the light and floral to the rich and spicy. The Regions and Their Whiskies Scotland's whisky-producing areas each have different profiles. Speyside is known for its sweet, fruity malts.

Highlands: Offers a range of styles, from peaty to heather-honey tastes. Islay is famous for its strong, smoky whiskies.

Lowlands: Typically lighter and softer. Campbeltown was once a whisky capital, known for its briny character. Tasting Like a Pro When drinking whiskey, it's all about the emotions. Look at the color, which can hint at age and cask type. Swirl the glass and note the 'legs' that run down the sides; slower legs can suggest a richer body. Smells for smells, or the 'nose'—this is where you'll find bits of fruit, spice, smoke, or wood. Take a small sip and let it fill your mouth, enjoying the 'palate' tastes. Finally, the 'finish' is the aftertaste that stays, showing more about the whisky's depth.

Pairing whisky with food: To enhance your tasting experience, mix whisky with food. Smoky whiskies pair well with rich foods or chocolate, whereas lighter whiskies complement seafood or cheese. Experiment and learn what tantalizes your taste buds.

Collecting Whisky: For those looking to start a collection, consider their uniqueness, age, and personal taste preferences. Limited versions or whiskey from closed companies can be particularly expensive.

Responsible Enjoyment: Remember, whisky drinking is about quality, not quantity. Drink responsibly and enjoy each dram for the expertise it represents. This guide is just the beginning of your whisky trip.

As you explore, you'll find that each bottle has a story, each brewery has a history, and each dram is a celebration of Scottish heritage.

Here's to your trip in the world of Scotch whisky—may it be as rich and fulfilling as the drink itself. Slàinte mhath! Learning the Art of Whisky Distilling While distilleries are the usual centers for learning about whiskey production, Glasgow offers other ways to study this skill. The Clydeside Distillery offers a thorough journey into the city's whisky history and the brewing process.

Additionally, The Glasgow Distillery is known for its award-winning drinks and offers views into current brewing techniques. In Glasgow, choosing whisky is part of the cultural experience. When ordering whisky in a pub, at bars like The Pot Still, with its huge range, you can simply ask the staff for a suggestion based on your taste preferences. A 'dram' is the traditional term for a helping of whiskey, and don't fear to ask about the pub's tasting flights for a more varied experience.

Popular Whisky Regions to Visit: Glasgow is an entrance to some of Scotland's most famous whiskey areas. Regional distilleries like Glengoyne and Auchentoshan are within reach and offer trips that showcase their unique production methods and flavors. Whisky Festivals to Attend Glasgow's Whisky Festival is a highlight, bringing together a wealth of whiskey from across Scotland.

Held at Hampden Park, it's a must-attend event for fans looking to try a wide range of whiskies and connect with experts. Where to Buy

Whisky as a Souvenir For a Unique Gift, visit The Whisky Shop in Buchanan Galleries, where you can find an extensive range of whiskey and experienced staff to help you choose the perfect bottle to take home. In conclusion, Glasgow is a lively place for whiskey fans.

Whether you're a seasoned expert or a curious newbie, the city's rich whisky culture offers a treasure trove of experiences that beckon you to raise a glass to the timeless spirit of Scotland. Slàinte mhath! (Good health!)

Best Places to Eat:

Glasgow offers a rich mix of food experiences, ranging from high-end eating to cozy neighborhood places.

Here's a better look at some of the best places to eat in this lively city:

The Ubiquitous Chip: This famous restaurant is a cornerstone of Glasgow's food scene, known for its unique approach to Scottish cooking. Nestled in the heart of the West End, it combines a visually appealing environment with a menu that taps into Scotland's rich larder.

Dishes like deer haggis and Isle of Gigha fish highlight local products and cocktails Bruich: With a Michelin star to its name, Cail Bruich offers a sophisticated eating experience that focuses on the food's quality and creativity.

Chef Lorna McNee continues to push cooking limits, making meals that are both modern and deeply rooted in ScottMother India is a local favorite, offering a mix of Indian and Scottish cooking customs. The restaurant is known for its creative food, transforming classic Indian meals into unique creations using Scottish products, all served in a lively and friendly environment.

Stravaigin, meaning 'to roam' in Gaelic, invites guests to experience world flavors using locally found products. The restaurant boasts a relaxed setting with a menu that's as suitable for a casual meal as it is for a special event, having foods that are both familiar and adventurous.

Five Marches This place, located near Kelvingrove Park, is known for its lively setting and a menu that emphasizes shared plates, making it ideal for group eating. The cooking style is Mediterranean-inspired, with meals that are perfect for any time of the day, from a relaxed brunch to a lively dinner.

Iasg: Specializing in seafood, Iasg (the Gaelic word for 'fish') is a celebration of Scotland's coastal wealth. The restaurant features a sleek, modern design and a menu that displays the best of Scottish seafood with a bit of international flair, making it a must-visit for seafood fans.

Gaucho Glasgow: In the heart of Glasgow, this Argentinian restaurant offers a taste of South America. Known for its quality cuts of beef, Gaucho provides a luxury eating experience, complete with stylish décor and a lively atmosphere perfect for both work meals and romantic nights.

La Pastina Deli: A gem for those wanting a casual bite, La Pastina Deli serves up a range of Italian deli classics, from freshly made pasta to delicious sandwiches and sweets. It's an ideal spot for a quick lunch or to pick up items for a fancy meal at home. These places not only show

Glasgow's food range but also its drive for quality and innovation in the cooking arts.

Whether you want a fancy eating experience or a casual meal, Glasgow's restaurant scene offers something that will please every taste.

Dietary Tips and Advice:

Glasgow, a lively city in Scotland, offers a diverse food scene that caters to a variety of dietary tastes and limits. Whether you're a vegan, vegetarian, gluten-free, or have other food needs, Glasgow has plenty to offer.

Research and Plan Ahead: Before you fly to Glasgow, take the time to fully research restaurants, bars, and stores that cater to your unique food needs. Utilize online resources such as HappyCow, TripAdvisor, and area food blogs to gather information about the best eating options available. Make note of any places that offer good diet menu items, and consider calling them in advance to ask about their options and make any necessary plans.

Explain Your Nutritional Needs: When eating out in Glasgow, it's important to explain your nutritional needs clearly to the restaurant staff. Most places are accustomed to meeting different food needs and are often willing to change meals to suit your tastes. Don't fear asking questions about products or cooking methods to ensure that your food meets your dietary limits.

Explore Vegan and Vegetarian Options: Glasgow boasts a thriving vegan and vegetarian food scene, with a wide range of places offering delicious plant-based meals. From vegan haggis to creative plant-based burgers, you'll find plenty of options to satisfy your tastes. To fully experience Glasgow's culinary choices, be sure to explore different places and try a variety of meals.

Enjoy traditional Scottish foods. While in Glasgow, don't miss the chance to try some traditional Scottish foods. Many places offer vegetarian versions of famous Scottish meals such as "neeps and tatties" (mashed turnips and potatoes) and "Scotch broth" (a rich vegetable soup). These meals provide a unique taste of Scottish food while also catering to your dietary requirements.

Visit Local Markets and Grocery Stores: One of the best ways to experience Glasgow's local food scene is by visiting local markets and grocery stores. The Barras Market and the city's farmers' markets offer a great selection of fresh fruit, snacks, and items for cooking your meals.

Exploring these markets can also provide insight into local food culture and customs. Be aware of hidden ingredients. When eating out, be vigilant about hidden ingredients in sauces, salads, and other foods that may not match your dietary needs. Ask restaurant workers about the products used in a particular dish and request changes if necessary. It's always better to be safe than sorry when it comes to your food limits.

Stay Hydrated: Glasgow's weather can be unpredictable, so it's important to stay hydrated, especially if you're exploring the city on foot. Carry a reusable water bottle with you and refill it at public water fountains or other places to ensure you stay hydrated throughout your travels.

Respect Local Customs and Traditions: As you explore Glasgow's food scene, take the time to respect local customs and traditions. For example, if you're coming during Burns Night, consider having a veggie version of the classic haggis to enjoy the event.

Embracing local traditions can improve your overall eating experience and help you understand Glasgow's rich cultural and history.

Seek local advice: Don't hesitate to ask the locals for suggestions on where to eat. Locals can provide useful insights into the best places to enjoy a meal that fits your food needs. Whether you're looking for a secret gem or a popular eating spot, locals can point you in the right direction and help you discover new culinary delights. Enjoy the experience.

Finally, remember to enjoy exploring Glasgow's food scene. Whether you're dining in a cozy pub, trying street food at a market, or enjoying a meal in a fine dining restaurant, Glasgow offers a unique culinary experience that caters to every palate. Soak up the sights, sounds, and tastes of the city and make unforgettable memories of your time in Glasgow.

In conclusion, Glasgow is a great location for visitors with food restrictions or tastes. With a little study and planning, you can enjoy a wide range of delicious and filling meals that cater to your needs. So pack your bags, prepare your taste buds, and get ready to enjoy the culinary wonders of Glasgow!

Festivals and Events

Glasgow Festival Fringe:

Glasgow, a city known for its rich cultural tapestry and lively arts scene, bursts into a variety of creativity each year with the Glasgow Festival Fringe. This chapter dives into the heart of this iconic festival, offering a comprehensive guide that reveals its history, unveils its lively highlights, and celebrates the diverse array of events that have solidified its status as a must-visit spot for culture fans worldwide.

History and origins: The origin of the Glasgow Festival Fringe can be traced back to the pioneering spirit of the Edinburgh Festival Fringe, which emerged in 1947 as a bold answer to the more formal Edinburgh International Festival. In the early 1980s, Glasgow bravely entered the world of fringe events, inspired by the groundbreaking success of its Edinburgh cousin. This move was driven by a desire to showcase Glasgow's growing arts and cultural scene, which was filled with raw talent and creative zeal. Since its beginning, the Glasgow Festival Fringe has grown, blooming into a cultural event that captivates artists, actors, and fans from every part of the world. At the heart of the Glasgow Festival Fringe lies its varied and diverse program, a lively fabric of artistic expression that covers a myriad of types and styles.

Whether you're a seasoned theater buff, a music fan, a dance enthusiast, or a student of the visual arts, the event caters to all tastes and preferences. The program is carefully selected to feature the best of local, national, and foreign talent, ensuring that every performance is a unique and memorable experience. One of the main features of the Glasgow Festival Fringe is its commitment to ease and equality. Venues are spread throughout the city, ranging from standard theaters to unusual places such as sheds, galleries, and even outdoor parks. This helps the event reach a larger audience and turn Glasgow into a lively hub of artistic activity.

In addition to standard shows, the Glasgow Festival Fringe also offers a range of participatory activities and classes. These can range from interactive stage shows that cross the lines between actor and audience to hands-on classes where participants can learn new skills and techniques from seasoned professionals. Another aspect of the event is its emphasis on showcasing rising talent. Many of the acts featured in the Glasgow Festival Fringe are up-and-coming artists who are making a name for themselves in the world of arts and culture.

This provides a stage for these artists to present their work to a larger public and gain important recognition. The Glasgow Festival Fringe is also known for its lively street entertainment scene. Throughout the festival, the streets of Glasgow come alive with buskers, street artists, and performers of all kinds, creating a lively and dynamic environment. This adds an element of surprise and energy to the event, as you never know what you might meet as you explore the city.

Overall, the Glasgow Festival Fringe is a celebration of creativity, variety, and artistic expression. Whether you're a seasoned festivalgoer or a first-time visitor, the festival offers a unique and engaging experience that will leave you inspired and thrilled. So, grab your tickets, explore the program, and get ready to find the magic of the Glasgow Festival Fringe.

Notable events and performances: One of the standout features of the Glasgow Festival Fringe is its reputation for presenting a fascinating blend of known artists and rising talents. This unusual mix ensures that tourists are exposed to a wide range of acts that push limits and question norms. Whether you're a fan of experimental theater, cutting-edge music, or boundary-pushing dance, the event offers a wealth of choices to fit every taste and preference. One of the festival's features is its focus on supporting inclusion and diversity in the arts.

Many of the acts featured in the Glasgow Festival Fringe handle important social issues and topics, providing a stage for artists to address real issues and prompt thought-provoking conversations. This dedication to socially conscious art has earned the event a reputation for promoting important conversation and thought.

In addition to standard shows, the Glasgow Festival Fringe also offers a variety of collaborative partnerships and unusual projects. These original shows often cross the lines between different art forms, creating engaging and changing experiences for viewers. From digital displays to participatory shows, the event invites artists to push the limits of their craft and explore new creative possibilities.

The "Best of the Fest" showcase, which features some of the festival's most amazing acts, is one of the festival's most anticipated events. This selected group of acts reflects the best of what the Glasgow Festival

Fringe has to offer, giving audiences a taste of the most exciting and original work in modern arts and culture.

Overall, the Glasgow Festival Fringe is a celebration of artistic greatness and creative innovation. Whether you're a seasoned arts fan or a curious newbie, the festival offers a wealth of opportunities to discover new talent, explore new ideas, and experience the changing power of the arts. So, involve yourself in the festival's varied program, accept the spirit of discovery, and prepare to be moved by the magic of the Glasgow Festival Fringe.

Notable events and performances: The Glasgow Festival Fringe is a melting pot of artistic expression, presenting a wide range of shows that push limits and question norms. Visitors can expect to see a mix of known singers and rising stars, with shows that span a wide range of types and styles.

From avant-garde stage shows to cutting-edge musical acts, the event prides itself on its original and diverse programming. One of the festival's features is its dedication to showing local talent. Many of the acts featured in the Glasgow Festival Fringe are made and performed by artists from Glasgow and the nearby areas, giving a stage for local creatives to present their work to a larger audience.

In addition to standard shows, the Glasgow Festival Fringe also offers a variety of participatory experiences and complex projects. These unique events cross the lines between artist and audience, creating memorable experiences that question perceptions. The "Fringe Sunday" street party, which takes place on the festival's final day, is one of the most anticipated events. This lively party includes live music, street acts, and food and drink stalls, providing a perfect end to the events.

Exploring the city Beyond the event sites, Glasgow offers a wealth of sights and experiences for tourists to enjoy. The city is famous for its beautiful architecture, with iconic sites such as the Glasgow Cathedral, the Riverside Museum, and the Kelvingrove Art Gallery and Museum showing the city's rich history and cultural heritage.

Glasgow is also home to a bustling nighttime scene, with a plethora of bars, clubs, and live music venues to discover. From traditional pubs serving up local brews to hip drink bars and underground clubs, there's something for everyone to enjoy after dark. Food lovers will enjoy Glasgow's culinary scene, which offers a diverse range of eating choices to fit every taste and price. From traditional Scottish fare to foreign food, the city's restaurants and cafes serve up a delicious array of dishes that reflect Glasgow's multicultural influences.

During the festival, Glasgow's streets come alive with a festive mood, with street musicians, buskers, and artists adding to the buzz. It's the perfect time to discover all that Glasgow has to offer, from its historic buildings to its lively cultural scene, and immerse yourself in the magic of this dynamic city.

Tips for Visitors Planning to Attend the Glasgow Festival Fringe?

Popular events at the Glasgow Festival Fringe tend to sell out quickly, so it's smart to book your tickets in advance. Check the festival's website or booking site for availability, and secure your spot early to avoid disappointment.

- Explore the Fringe Guide: The Glasgow Festival Fringe offers a thorough guide that lists all the events, shows, and places. Take the time to read the book and plan your schedule in advance.

- Highlight the events you're interested in, and make a plan to make the most of your time at the fair.
- Embrace the Unexpected: The Glasgow Festival Fringe is known for its unusual mix of acts, ranging from the classic to the avant-garde.
- Don't be afraid to step out of your comfort zone and try something new. You might find a secret gem or a new favorite act.
- Arrive Early: Arriving early for your chosen events can ensure you get a good spot and avoid the last-minute rush.
- Give yourself plenty of time to travel the city and find the place, especially if it's your first time attending the event.
- Stay open: While it's great to have a plan, it's also important to stay open. Events may run longer than planned, or you may come across something unexpected that catches your eye.
- Allow yourself the freedom to stray from your plan and discover new chances as they appear.

Stay Connected: Follow the Glasgow Festival Fringe on social media and sign up for their email to stay updated on the latest news and events. This can help you stay up-to-date on any changes to the plan or new events that may interest you.

Immerse Yourself in the Culture: The Glasgow Festival Fringe is about more than just the shows; it's also about the city's culture and vibe. Take the time to experience Glasgow's lively streets, soak up the local culture, and connect with fellow festivalgoers. For those wanting to attend the Glasgow Festival Fringe, there are a few tips to keep in mind. It's wise to book tickets in advance for popular events, as they tend to sell out quickly.

Additionally, it's worth studying the fringe guide and planning your schedule in advance to make the most of your time at the event. Finally, don't be afraid to step out of your comfort zone and try something new; the Glasgow Festival Fringe is all about finding and exploring.

In conclusion, the Glasgow Festival Fringe is a celebration of talent, variety, and innovation. Whether you're a seasoned festivalgoer or a first-time visitor, the festival offers a unique and amazing experience that displays the best of Glasgow's arts and culture scene. So, mark your calendars and get ready to immerse yourself in the magic of the Glasgow Festival Fringe!

Hogmanay Celebrations:

In Scotland, Hogmanay is more than just a night of revelry; it's a time-honored holiday deep in history and rich in customs. The roots of the word "Hogmanay" are unknown, with ideas ranging from Norse, Gaelic, and French elements. Regardless of its origin, Hogmanay is Scotland's way of accepting the New Year with open arms and a warm heart. Scotland's Hogmanay parties are famous worldwide for their festive spirit and lively atmosphere. The parties last for several days, with Edinburgh's famous Street Party bringing thousands of tourists from around the world.

However, Glasgow's Hogmanay events are equally lively and offer a unique experience for tourists looking to ring in the New Year in style.

Glasgow's Hogmanay: A City Alive with Celebration Glasgow, known for its friendly locals and lively cultural scene, comes alive during the Hogmanay events. The city's streets are covered with festive decorations, and the air is filled with the sound of laughter and music. From traditional ceilidh dances to trendy shows, there is something for everyone in Glasgow on Hogmanay. One of the highlights of Glasgow's Hogmanay celebrations is the torchlight procession, where thousands of people march through the city streets holding burning lanterns.

This spectacular event ends with a beautiful fireworks show, lighting up the night sky and marking the start of the new year. Events and activities Torchlight Procession is a must-see event, bringing together locals and tourists alike to join in this old custom. The parade starts at George Square and makes its way through the city streets, providing a stunning visual show.

Concerts and live music: Glasgow is famous for its music scene, and Hogmanay is no exception. The city hosts a range of shows and live music events, starring both local talent and foreign acts. From traditional Scottish music to modern hits, there is something for everyone to enjoy. Hogmanay Parties For those looking to dance the night away, Glasgow's Hogmanay parties are not to be missed.

Many bars and clubs host special events, providing a lively atmosphere and plenty of opportunities to party with fellow partygoers. During Hogmanay, families traveling with children will find plenty of family-friendly events to enjoy in Glasgow. From storytelling groups to arts and crafts classes, there is no lack of fun and festive activities for all ages.

Glasgow Hogmanay Celebrations 2024: Event Listings and Upcoming Events

As you plan your visit to Glasgow for the Hogmanay celebrations in

2024, here are some of the exciting events and activities to look forward to:

Torchlight Procession Date: December 30, 2024, Location: George Square to Glasgow Green Description: Join thousands of players as they march through the city streets holding lights, creating a stunning visual show. The parade ends in a big finale at Glasgow Green, where a spectacular fireworks show lights up the night sky.

George Square Street Party Date: December 31, 2024 Location: George Square Description: Experience the festive mood of Glasgow's Street Party, featuring live music, DJ sets, and traditional Scottish dances. Enjoy food and drink from local sellers as you celebrate with locals and fellow tourists.

Concerts and live music: Various dates and locations: Throughout December 2024 Description: Glasgow's music scene comes alive during Hogmanay, with a range of shows and live music events taking place across the city. From traditional Scottish music to modern hits, there's something for everyone to enjoy.

Hogmanay Parties: Various Locations: Throughout Glasgow Description: Join in the Hogmanay activities at one of Glasgow's many bars and clubs, which host special events and parties to ring in the New Year. Dance the night away and celebrate with friends old and new.

Family-Friendly Activities Various Locations: Throughout Glasgow Description: Families going with children can enjoy a range of family-friendly activities, including storytelling groups, arts and crafts classes, and outdoor entertainment. These events offer a fun and lively way for families to celebrate together. For the most up-to-date information on event dates, places, and purchasing details, check the official Glasgow City Council website and local event listings closest to the date.

As you prepare to join Glasgow's Hogmanay events, consider these expert tips to make the most of your experience:

- 1. Plan Ahead: Book your accommodations well in advance, as Glasgow tends to get busy during the Hogmanay events. Consider staying in the city center for easy access to the events. Transportation: Plan your transportation in advance, especially if you're attending events in various places. Glasgow's public transportation system is dependable, but cabs and ridesharing services can be more handy, especially late at night.
-
- 2. Dress warmly. Weather: Glasgow's weather can be uncertain, so dress warmly and be prepared for rain. Layering is key, as temperatures can drop greatly in the evening. Comfortable Shoes: Wear comfortable shoes, as you'll likely be walking and standing for long periods of time while exploring the city's events.
-
- 3. Experience the local culture. Ceilidh Dancing: For a truly Scottish experience, join in on a traditional ceilidh dance. These lively dances are easy to learn and are a fun way to immerse yourself in the local culture. Try Scottish Cuisine: Sample traditional Scottish foods and drinks, such as haggis, neeps, and tatties, along with a dram of whisky to toast the New Year.
-
- 4. Safety Tips: Stay in groups. When visiting the city at night, especially after the main events have finished, stay in groups and avoid badly lit or new areas. Watch for pickpockets. Be aware of

- your belongings in crowded places, and keep valuables safe.
- 5. Enjoy the fireworks. Best viewing spots: For the best views of the fireworks, head to high places such as Glasgow Green or the Clyde Arc (Squinty Bridge). Arrive early to gain a good spot.

Be Respectful: Remember to be respectful of local residents and the environment by dumping litter properly and following any directions from event staff. Follow these expert tips to make the most of your Hogmanay parties in Glasgow and create unforgettable memories of this unique Scottish holiday.

Commonwealth Games:

The Glasgow 2014 Commonwealth Games will be praised for their amazing success, with 71 countries and regions participating across 17 sports during the 11-day event from July 23 to August 4. From the meticulousness of lawn bowls to the exciting combats of boxing, judo, and wrestling, and from the adrenaline-pumping athletics and cycling track events to the elegant displays of gymnastics, Glasgow displayed a spectacular summer of sports.

Additionally, the city featured a range of cultural and artistic events for all participants. The sports program included 17 games: aquatics (diving, swimming), athletics, badminton, boxing, cycling (mountain bike, road, track), gymnastics (artistic, rhythmic), hockey, judo, lawn bowls, netball, rugby sevens, shooting, squash, table tennis, triathlon, weightlifting, and wrestling.

Notably, the Games also featured the biggest amount of Para-Sports Medals in Commonwealth Games history, with 22 medal events, including the original Triathlon Mixed Relay event and the first Para-Sport Cycling (Track) event. Most sports were held in three small site groups within Glasgow, with the shooting events taking place at Carnoustie, diving in Edinburgh, and cycling matches at Strathclyde Country Park. The bidding process for the 2014 Commonwealth Games began on February 24, 2006, and ended with Glasgow emerging as the winner on November 9, 2007, gaining 47 votes.

The pick of Glasgow as the host city for the XX version of the Games was made by the General Assembly of the Commonwealth Games Federation at a meeting in Sri Lanka. The Glasgow 2014 Commonwealth Games created a new standard for the Commonwealth sports movement and set goals for holding big events in Scotland. The Games earned major praise for Glasgow, the host city, which warmly welcomed athletes and tourists during Scotland's largest-ever sports and cultural event.

The large public sector funds given to the Games guaranteed that the entire event was delivered to exceptionally high standards, with the stadiums and Athletes' Village generally recognized for their quality. Glasgow 2014 also enjoyed unique local and national support, selling approximately 1.3 million tickets and getting steady commitment from Games Partners and sponsors.

Aligned with the Commonwealth Games Federation's core values, Glasgow 2014 was praised by the Equality Network for setting "a new benchmark for inclusivity." Notably, Glasgow 2014 became the first sports mega-event group abroad to print its approach to human rights. The Opening and Closing Ceremonies were particularly praised for their celebration of variety, with Amnesty International praising 'The Glasgow Kiss' for its role in breaking down boundaries. A pioneering relationship with UNICEF raised £5 million to help children throughout Scotland and the Commonwealth.

Celebrities invited watchers to give via text during an emotionally moving call at the Opening Ceremony, creating a sense of unity and giving. The 2026 Commonwealth Games will be held in Victoria, Australia, from March 17 to 29. This version of the Games will follow a unique multi-city plan, spreading events across five regional hubs: Melbourne, Ballarat, Bendigo, Geelong, and Gippsland. This method aims to showcase the variety and cultural wealth of these areas. The sports program will feature 20 sports and 26 categories, including fully combined parasports.

Notable sports include aquatics, athletics, cricket, cycling, and new features like golf and coastal rowing. Each hub will host different sports, creating a spread-fair vibe throughout. For example, Ballarat will host athletics and paraathletes; Bendigo will cover lawn bowls and netball; and Geelong will see a range of sports, including aquatics and the launch of golf at the Commonwealth Games (Commonwealth Sport) (Victorian Institute of Sport). For visitors hoping to attend the Games, it's wise to book housing and transport well in advance, especially in these regional hubs. Each site offers unique cultural and historical sights, complementing the sports events with local gatherings and activities.

Tickets for the events will likely go on sale closer to the Games date, and it's suggested to regularly check official sites for details and early bird deals. The Commonwealth Games in Victoria not only aim to provide an excellent sports experience but also to leave a permanent memory. Infrastructure improvements for the Games are planned to help the communities long after, including turning athlete towns into cheap homes and upgrading local sports facilities (Victorian Institute of Sport). For the latest changes and thorough information, keeping an eye on the official Victoria 2026 Commonwealth Games website is advised.

Other Noteworthy Events:

Glasgow, a city alive with culture, history, and an array of events, offers a plethora of activities that range from music festivals to traditional Scottish celebrations. This chapter explores a variety of holidays and events in Glasgow, giving insights into their cultural importance and offering advice on when to attend these gatherings.

1. Celtic Connections Dates: Late January to early February Celtic Connections is one of the UK's biggest winter music events, featuring folk, roots, and world music. The event runs over 18 days, starting in late January. It features more than 2,000 acts from around the world performing at various venues in Glasgow. The event not only celebrates Scottish music but also welcomes a variety of foreign influences, making it a lively and rewarding cultural experience.

2. Glasgow International Comedy Festival Dates: March Laughter fills the air in Glasgow every March during the Glasgow International Comedy Festival, the biggest event of its kind in Europe. Venues throughout the city host stand-up comedy acts, sketch shows, and funny theater, drawing both local stars and famous international comics. This event offers a perfect mix of humor that can cater to all tastes, whether you prefer dry wit or slapstick.

3. West End Festival Dates: The West End Festival, Glasgow's biggest cultural event, takes place in June. It turns the West End into a busy arts and culture hub with a mix of music, shows, performances, talks, trips, and especially the famous parade day. Streets and places buzz with activities, making it a happy time to explore the creativity and artistic style of the area.

4. Merchant City Festival Dates: Late July to early August Celebrated in one of Glasgow's most historic areas, the Merchant City Festival spans several days and offers street arts, music, theater, food, and drink. It highlights the cultural wealth of the Merchant City and serves as a platform for local and international artists. This event is particularly known for its lively environment and the variety of acts.

5. Glasgow Doors Open Days Festival Dates: September The Glasgow Doors Open Days Festival is part of a national event that gives free access to buildings that are not usually open to the public or would normally charge an entry fee. Held yearly in September, this event offers a unique chance to explore Glasgow's rich historical history through guided trips, talks, and events. It's an excellent way to dig into the city's past and build wonders.

6. Glasgow Film Festival dates: February to March The Glasgow Film Festival is a yearly event celebrating the art of film, held between February and March. The festival shows an unusual mix of films from all over the world, running from popular hits to independent art house movies, documentaries, and more. It's a must-visit for movie fans looking to catch some unique and inspiring films.

7. Piping Live! Dates: August: Glasgow hosts 'Piping Live! a week-long piping event that features some of the world's best bagpipers and

traditional bands. Occurring in August, the event includes shows, competitions, and street performances, culminating in the famous World Pipe Band Championships. This event not only celebrates Scottish pipe customs but also groups varied musical styles inspired by global cultures.

8. Hogmanay Dates: December 31st While Edinburgh's Hogmanay gets much attention, Glasgow also offers a lively New Year's party. Glasgow's Hogmanay includes street parties, bands, traditional Scottish music, and the famous midnight fireworks. It's a lively event that brings together locals and tourists to welcome the new year with joy and fun.

Each of these events shows different parts of Glasgow's rich cultural mix, giving guests a complete experience of the city's lively and diverse cultural scene. Whether you're a music lover, a film buff, or someone who appreciates fine art and history, Glasgow's annual festivals and events provide something for everyone.

Practical Information

Getting Around Glasgow:

Getting Around Glasgow: Going around Glasgow on foot is the best option. Many of the best things to do are located in the city center, and the grid plan makes it very easy to travel. However, several sites are located on the outskirts, necessitating the use of the public transportation system or a car. Black cabs are also available, and you can hail them on the streets or find them at taxi stops (or lines) throughout the city center. If you took a plane into Glasgow International Airport (GLA), you can take a train, bus, cab, or rental car the 10 miles into the city center.

The fastest way to reach the city center via public transportation is the Glasgow Airport Express service 500 bus, which takes 15 minutes. Tickets cost 8.50 pounds (or about $11) for adults and 4.50 pounds (around $6) for kids. If you plan on living in the city center, getting around on foot is your best bet. Its grid plan makes getting lost nearly impossible, and many of the best sights are also gathered here.

Bus: Bus Greater Glasgow covers the center of Glasgow as well as Greater Glasgow, from Loch Lomond to the northwest and Lanarkshire to the southeast. Bus passes can be bought in numerous quantities: a single fare, a first-day ticket for a day of unlimited travel, and a first-week ticket for seven days of unlimited travel. Fares start at about 2 pounds (around $2.50) and are decided by distance (a zone system). First Bus has more than 950 buses covering more than 80 lines; timings vary greatly by route and day of the week, with buses usually running from around 6 a.m. to after 11. p.m. on weekends on major lines.

On its website, First Bus provides a list of the top sites and related bus lines.Hop-on, hop-off tourist buses are another choice for visiting the city's top sites. For more information, please check out our list of the best Scottish tours. First Bus Subway: The Strathclyde Partnership for Transport (SPT) is Glasgow's efficient bus, boat, and subway system. The underground, known as Clockwork Orange, has two circle lines, one running clockwise and the other running counterclockwise.

Tickets can be bought at the train stops; a single, one-way ticket costs less than 2 pounds (around $2.50). Subways run from 6:30 a.m. to around 11:30 p.m. every day except Sunday, when they run from 10 a.m. to around 6 p.m. During peak times, trains arrive every 4 minutes; at other times, they come roughly 6 to 8 minutes apart. Because some of Glasgow's sights are located on the outskirts, you might want a car for your stay. (Buses and subway trains can also take you to the outer-lying sites.) Rent them at the Glasgow airport or find several companies in the city.

Keep in mind that Glaswegians drive on the left, and "permit parking" signs mean permit parking only. If you park in one of these places without a ticket, your car could be towed. While a legal driving license is needed, a foreign driving pass is not. Taxi: The U.K.'s famous black cabs can be found in Glasgow. Hail one on the street, or find them in cab ranks throughout the city.

Several companies, including Glasgow Taxis and Hampden Cars, also allow you to book through their sites or smartphone apps. Uber also runs in Glasgow. Your cab ride shouldn't surpass about 15 pounds (around $19), but keep in mind that an extra surcharge will be added if you ride late at night or early in the morning. Glasgow Taxis Hampden CarsUberBikeLike many towns around the U.K. Glasgow, like elsewhere, has a bike-sharing system that allows people to travel the city on two wheels. Prices usually range from about 1 pound (around $1.30) for a 30-minute trip to 10 pounds (about $13) for a full day of entry.

Weather and Best Time to Visit:

Glasgow, Scotland's biggest city and a cultural hub in the west of the country, hasn't always enjoyed the best image. However, in recent years, this former industrial city has done a lot to improve its image and attract tourists from across the UK and around the world. In particular, the regeneration of the River Clyde region has fundamentally changed the way the city looks, lives, and works, making it far more appealing as a vacation location than it used to be. Still, a couple of things haven't changed. One is that the locals will be the same modest and down-to-earth types they have always been. Another is that the weather in Glasgow can play a big role in picking when to visit.

Western Scotland's reputation for uncertain weather is well-deserved, and no matter what time of year you visit, you can expect to face some wet weather when you visit Scotland. But that's no reason not to go. At worst, the colder weather just gives you a reason to curl up next to the log fires in some of the city's more friendly bars and enjoy a dram of whiskey. Plus, with some great tourist sites to see, it's worth facing the Scottish weather to see what Glasgow has to offer, whether you visit in the peak summer time or in the winter season.

Chances are, you'll have a wonderful time either way. You'll have an even better time if you drop off your bags at a Bounce luggage room in Glasgow. Leave your things behind, but make sure you bring a rain jacket when you visit any part of Scotland.Summer in Glasgow The summer weather in Glasgow can be beautiful, with long days and warm temperatures making it ideal for exploring everything the city has to offer. However, as with the rest of Scotland, there's also a chance that you'll face some rain during your stay. That said, the chances of having wet weather are smaller in Glasgow than in other parts of the country, especially in the Highlands.

And even if it does rain, it's unlikely to last for long. So don't let a little bit of water stop you from enjoying all that Glasgow has to offer during the summer months. Summer is certainly the hottest time of the year, with average temperatures sitting at a nice 61°F (16°C). However, it's not rare for the temperature to rise above 68°F (20°C), making it nice for going around and visiting the city. Of course, if you want to make the most of the good weather, there are plenty of outdoor things to enjoy in Glasgow.

The Riverside Museum is a great choice, especially on a sunny day when you can walk along the River Clyde. Or, for something a bit more active, take a hike up to the Cathkin Braes, where you'll be rewarded with fantastic views of the city. Because of Glasgow's northerly location, summer brings long daylight hours, which, paired with the relatively average high temperature, makes the summer season ideal for outdoor culture events in the city.

If you choose to visit Glasgow during the beautiful summer days and warm weather, you can enjoy gatherings like the World Pipe Band Championships and the Glasgow Mela, as well as a host of other smaller events, including the Highland Games. You could even head out of the city and make the hour and a half trip to Scotland's capital to see the Edinburgh Military Tattoo and the Edinburgh Fringe Festival, one of the biggest performing arts events in the world.

Visit Glasgow during the summer, and you'll be able to enjoy high temperatures, great fairs, and interesting cultural events. However, summer is most definitely a high tourist season, so don't expect to have the city to yourself. Additionally, room prices will be higher during the high season than at most other times of the year. If you want to avoid the dark days of the winter months, enjoy live music, and experience higher temperatures, summer is probably the best time to visit Glasgow, with July usually being the hottest month of the year. But if you'd prefer to avoid the biggest prices and crowds that come with sunny days, it might be worth packing your rain gear and considering another time of year.

Fall in Glasgow: After the busy summer season, things tend to quiet down a little in Glasgow in the fall. The weather also starts to cool off, making it a great time to visit if you don't mind a little bit of chill in the air. Average temperatures in September and October are around 55°F (13°C), with the odd surge into the 60°F (16°C) range in early fall. November sees temperatures drop a bit further, with an average of 48°F (9°C). However, even though it's getting colder, there's still plenty to do in Glasgow during the fall months. One of the best things about visiting Glasgow in the fall is that you'll escape the crowds that come with tourist season.

However, that doesn't mean nothing is going on in the city. In fact, November is when Glasgow comes alive with several events and concerts. The first two weeks of November see the return of the Glasgow International Jazz Festival, which features some of the biggest names in jazz from all over the world. And at the end of the month, you can enjoy the Glasgow Film Festival, which features pictures from around the world. If you're looking for a quieter trip, fall is also a great time to take advantage of Glasgow's many museums and art galleries.

With fewer people around, you'll be able to enjoy them at your own pace without having to think about groups. Pack your coats and jackets when you visit Glasgow in the fall, as the weather can be quite cool. You might also want to pack an umbrella, as November is one of the rainiest months of the year.Winter in Glasgow: Although winter is the coldest time of year to visit Glasgow, it's also one of the most beautiful. December sees temperatures drop to an average of 41°F (5°C), with highs only hitting about 50°F (10°C). January and February are even colder.

However, just because it's cold doesn't mean there's nothing to do in Glasgow during the winter months. In fact, winter is when the city springs to life, with tons of great holiday activities to do around town. One of the best things about visiting Glasgow in winter is that you'll be able to enjoy the holiday season in all its glory. Christmas markets pop up all over the city, and you can even ice skate in Glasgow's very own Winter Wonderland.

If you're looking for something a bit more low-key, winter is also a great time to visit Glasgow's many museums and art galleries. With fewer people around, you'll be able to enjoy them at your own pace without having to think about groups. As well as Christmas, Glasgow is famous for its Hogmanay party, the lively Scottish New Year's event that is a highlight of the low season. Many people come to the city for the Christmas and New Year's period, so hotel prices will usually be higher around this time. Also, don't forget that one of the most quintessentially Scottish events of the year, Burns Night, takes place in January.

This celebration of Scotland's national poet, Robert Burns, has grown over the years into a celebration of Scottish culture, with all the music, poems, food, and drink that suggests. If you're looking to engage yourself in Scottish culture, this may be the best time to visit Glasgow, even if you will face a lower average temperature than at other times of the year. The celebration of the life and works of Robert Burns is an event not to be missed.When packing for a winter trip to Glasgow, be sure to bring along your best clothes.

Temperatures can drop below freezing, so you'll need boots, hats, scarves, and gloves to stay comfortable. You might also want to pack an umbrella, as December is one of the rainiest months of the year.Spring in Glasgow: Although spring is a great time to visit Glasgow, it's also one of the busiest times of the year. The weather starts to warm up in March, with normal temperatures of 48°F (9°C) and highs getting into the 70°F (21°C) range. April and May are even warmer, with values of 55°F (13°C) and 61°F (16°C), respectively.

One of the best things about visiting Glasgow in the spring is that you'll be able to enjoy the beautiful weather. This is a great time to explore Glasgow's many parks, as they'll be in full bloom. You might also want to take advantage of the warmer weather by doing some sightseeing outside of the city center. Although the crowds do pick up in the spring, Glasgow tourist sites such as museums and galleries are typically not as busy as they are in the summer.

In your valuable shots, there are fewer lines and fewer people. When packing for a spring trip to Glasgow, be sure to bring along some light clothes. The weather can be quite changeable at this time of year, so it's always good to have a jacket or sweater on hand. You might also want to pack an umbrella, as April also sees its fair share of rain.

In addition to being a great time to enjoy the weather, late spring is also a busy time for events in Glasgow. The Glasgow International Jazz Festival takes place in late June, while the West End Festival runs from early June to early July. Hotel prices will usually be higher around these times, so be sure to book in advance if you're planning on coming during peak season.

When is the best time to visit Glasgow for you? Anytime you plan to visit Scotland, you can't discount the part the weather will play in your schedule. Glasgow most definitely experiences four seasons, sometimes all in one day, so no matter when you visit this coastal city, you'll need to be prepared for just about everything the weather can throw at you. On the plus side, Glasgow natives have learned how to deal with the changeable nature of Scotland's weather.

No matter what time of year you visit, you'll find plenty of things to keep you busy both indoors and out. Glasgow is also backed by some spectacular scenery, and if you want to make the most of it, the sunny days of summer are probably the best time to do it. This weather, combined with all of the great events in the city, makes summer an attractive choice. Spring, fall, and even winter all have their own charms, so don't ignore these seasons. The parties and events in Glasgow are capable of warming up even the coldest months of the year, so if you want to experience the best of Scottish culture, winter can be a great time to visit. Often, what you choose to bring on a trip to Scotland can make or break your trip.

You'll need to prepare for all kinds of weather, but to make sure you don't get weighed down, drop off your bags at a Bounce luggage storage in Glasgow. That way, you'll be prepared for whatever the weather throws at you.

Safety Tips:

When planning a visit to Glasgow, it's important to consider safety. Glasgow is usually a safe city, but like any big area, certain steps should be taken to ensure a nice and secure stay.

General safety tips: Glasgow, the biggest city in Scotland, offers a rich cultural scene and ancient importance. To ensure your safety, protect your values. Petty thefts, such as pickpocketing, are widespread, especially in busy areas and public transport hubs. Use anti-theft bags, or keep jewelry in the inner pockets of tightly tied bags.

Neighborhoods: Consider staying in places like the West End, Merchant City, or Shawlands, which are known for their safety and lively local life. Night Safety: Be careful at night, especially in nightlife-heavy places like Sauchiehall Street. It's recommended to move in groups and stay in well-lit, crowded places.

PRACTICAL INFORMATION

Public transport is efficient and safe during the day. However, it's wise to be more watchful at night. Specific areas to avoid: Some places pose higher risks and should generally be avoided, especially at night.Higher Crime Areas: Places like Pollokshields and Springburn have higher crime rates. To reduce the risk, avoid these locations.

Avoiding Scams: Stay alert for travel scams, which often involve distraction methods used by groups working together to steal.

Emergency Preparedness: Knowing how to react in a situation is crucial. Emergency Contacts: Always have the numbers for local emergency services (999 for police, fire, and ambulance) and non-emergency police assistance (101).

Trip insurance: Ensure that your trip insurance covers theft, loss, and medical situations. Familiarize yourself with the terms. Cultural Sensitivity and Local Interactions: Respecting local practices and connecting politely with locals not only enhances safety but also improves your trip experience.

Local Advice: Always ask your hotel or local friends for safety tips and suggestions on areas to avoid. Cultural Awareness: Understanding local rules and social etiquette is crucial to avoiding mistakes. By following these guidelines and staying informed, your visit to Glasgow can be both safe and enjoyable, allowing you to fully experience the rich Scottish history and lively life of this historic city.

Useful Glasgow Phrases:

When visiting Glasgow, involving yourself in the local lingo can improve your trip experience and help you connect with residents. Glasgow's accent, known locally as "Glaswegian," includes unique words and statements that might sound strange to non-locals.

Here's a list of useful words that tourists can use to handle talks in this bustling Scottish city.

Greetings and Basic Interactions: "How are you?" This is a popular way to say "How are you?" in Glaswegian. It's friendly and relaxed. "Aye" means "yes." It's one of the most commonly used words in Scotland. "Naw" simply says "no." "Cheers": While it is commonly known as a drinking toast, in Glasgow it also means "thanks.At shops or restaurants, "Can I have a look?" when you want to take a closer look at something, perhaps in a shop. "Whaur's the bog?" It's useful to know if you're looking for toilets. "Bogs" is a slang term for toilets. "That's braw!" means "That's great!" It is useful when praising food or services.

Getting Around: "Whit's the wiy tae?" translates to "What's the way to…" It is helpful when asking for directions. "Is this the richest bus fur?" means "Is this the right bus for…" Crucial for handling public transport. Making small talk, "It's a dreich day, isn't it?" Referring to the weather, "dreich" describes a dark, bleak, or dull day, which isn't uncommon in Glasgow! "Yer fae…" means "You're from…" A good conversation starter if you're curious about someone's roots.

Common Courtesies "Ta" is another way to say "thanks." It's short and used loosely. "Dinnae fash yersel" means "Don't worry about it." It's a comforting phrase to use if someone apologizes to you for a small mistake.

Expressing enjoyment or approval, "Pure, dead brilliant!" is an exciting way to show that something is excellent or amazing. "This is some manky weather, eh?" "Manky" means bad or nasty. It's a funny and nice way to comment on bad weather. See you later!" means "See you later! "A usual way to say goodbye. "Haste ye back" is often used to tell people to return soon. It demonstrates kindness and a desire for a swift return.

Learning these words can help you navigate Glasgow more effectively and perhaps even impress a few locals with your understanding of their accents. Remember, Scots are usually very proud of their history and language, and they enjoy any effort guests make to accept.

Hidden Gems

Hidden Gems in Glasgow:

Glasgow has many amazing places and sights for you to get lost in. However, if you go a bit deeper and look a little harder, there are secret gems in and around the city that you shouldn't miss, as they offer the same (and sometimes even better) experience!

The Glasgow Mural Trail, which began with a single artwork in 2008, has since grown to include more than 30 unique pieces of street art. Brightening up dark streets and unused walls, the diverse selection of paintings, all created by local artists, has been marked as a path for tourists to follow, helping them to discover the best shops and restaurants in the city center while enjoying the creative.

The entire attraction is free and open to anyone who wants to be amazed by the numerous paintings along the trail, ranging from the Osborne Street picture of Scottish actor and comedian Sir Billy Connolly to the famous Glasgow Panda on Mitchell Lane.

How to get there Nestled in the heart of Glasgow, the Mural Trail is a lively testament to the city's creative pulse. To start on this urban adventure, simply make your way to the heart of the city. If you're coming in, Glasgow Airport is your entrance, with easy transport links to the city. For those coming by train, Glasgow Central Station is your stop, putting you just a stone's throw away from the first painting. And if you're driving, parking spots are abundant near George Square, a great starting point for the trail. The

Best Time to Visit: The paintings splashed across the city's buildings, are on display come rain or shine. However, the best time to visit would be during the spring or summer months, when the Scottish weather is more agreeable. The daylight lasts longer, giving you extra time to walk through the streets and admire the arts. Aim for a weekday visit to avoid the weekend crowds, and you'll find the paintings waiting for you, free from the rush and bustle.

Safety Tips: As you walk the Mural Trail, safety is simple. The road is well-trodden and friendly for solo travelers or groups alike. Keep an eye on your things, as you would in any city, and wear comfortable shoes for the walk. The paintings are in public areas, so there's no need to travel anywhere that feels dangerous. And remember, Glasgow's people are known for their friendliness and helpfulness, so you're in good company.

Photography Tips: Now, to catch these wonders, here are some tips: early morning light: For the shooters out there, early morning pro provides a soft light that can make the colors of the paintings pop.

Golden hour: Alternatively, the golden hour before sunset brings a warm glow that can add a dramatic effect to your shots. Wide-Angle Lens: A wide-angle lens is your best friend on the Mural Trail, allowing you to catch the full beauty of the artworks, even in small lanes. Look Up: Some of the best pieces are high above street level, so don't forget to look up and find those secret gems.

Reflections: For a unique perspective, use shop windows or puddles to record reflections of the paintings after rain. With these tips in hand, you're set to discover and record the Glasgow Mural Trail, a celebration of color and culture on the canvas of the city. Happy looking!

Spiral Hill Flagpole

On the edges of Glasgow's city heart, a twisting circle walk on a green hillock leads to a mast topped by a tall metal flag. Officially called the "Spiral Hill Flagpole," the green knoll is popularly known as the "Plean Street Pyramid" or the "Blawarthill Ziggurat." Despite its fascinating presence, the site itself remains wrapped in mystery, missing any markers or statements about its beginnings.

Historical evidence and the best guesses of local scholars say that in the late 1800s, the place was home to Blawarthill Farm. As the city grew, the green area was turned into two 20-story tower blocks in the 1960s. Following their destruction in 2010, it is thought that the rubble was compressed into the mound on which the flagpole now stands.

How to get there: The Spiral Hill Flagpole, also known as the "Plean Street Pyramid" or "Blawarthill Ziggurat," is a secret gem tucked away on the edges of Glasgow's busy city center. To reach this fascinating spot, you'll want to head towards Plean Street in Garscadden. If you're coming by train, Garscadden station is your nearest stop. From there, it's just a short walk south to the flagpole. For those who prefer a beautiful walk, the old Lanarkshire and Dumbartonshire Railway path, now a pedestrian and bike path, runs right past the hill and provides a relaxed approach.

The Best Time to Visit: While the Spiral Hill Flagpole can be viewed year-round, the best views are to be had on a clear day when the vast vistas across the west of Glasgow can be fully enjoyed. There's no specific season that's best for going, but a warm day will certainly improve the experience. The spot is an open green area, so it's available at any time.

Safety Tips: The Spiral Hill Flagpole stands in a public urban green area and is usually considered safe to visit. However, as with any city trip, it's smart to stay aware of your surroundings. The area is open, and the view is good, making it a safe spot for solo tourists or groups. There's no need for special safety steps beyond what common sense means, like keeping an eye on personal belongings.

Photography Tips: Capturing the spirit of the Spiral Hill Flagpole in a picture can be a satisfying task.

Here are some tips to help you get the best shots:

Use the spiral path. The slightly rising spiral path not only gets you to the top, but it also offers a unique frame device for your pictures. Time of Day: For scenery photos, visit during the early morning or late afternoon, when the light is warmer and more appealing.

Seasonal Changes: Consider coming during different seasons to capture the changing scenery and skies that Scotland is famous for. With these tips, you're all set to discover and capture the Spiral Hill Flagpole, a curious landmark with a story wrapped in mystery. Whether you're a local or a tourist, this spot offers a peaceful escape from the city's hustle and a chance to ponder the layers of history beneath your feet.

Provan Gas Works

Provan Gas Works, dominated by two tall blue metal gasometers that rise above the nearby post-industrial scenery, is practically unknown to tourists, yet among locals it is considered an important landmark. Once an important facility for Britain's energy needs, privatization of the UK gas industry under the Thatcher government during the 1980s caused the fall of the facility.

Now largely unmanned and used solely for gas storage, the twin gasometers are visible from the two freeways connecting Glasgow and Edinburgh, thus making an interurban entrance. This high point has led to the display of huge posters advertising the city, often filled with typical Glaswegian comedy.

How to get there: Provan Gas Works, a relic of Glasgow's industrial might, sits tall between the Blackhill, Blochairn, Germiston, and Provanmill areas. To find this industrial giant, you can travel to 313 Blochairn Road, Glasgow, G21 2RX1. If you're using public transport, the nearest train stops are Bellgrove and Alexandra Parade. From there, a short bus ride will take you to the gas station. For those driving, the M8 and M80 freeways provide a straight route, making the gas holders an obvious feature as you enter the city's central area.

The Best Time to Visit: While there's no official 'best time' to visit the Provan Gas Works, the opinion among locals says that a clear day is ideal for understanding the sheer scale of the gasometers. They are particularly striking when the sun throws shadows, accentuating their industrial architecture. The spot is available throughout the year, but coming during daylight hours will ensure you get the best views and photographs.

Safety Tips: Because Provan Gas Works is an industrial site, guests must be aware of their surroundings. While the area is not known for specific dangers, it's always smart to stay within public access areas. Keep an eye out for any operating tools or cars. Keep a safe distance from buildings unless they are marked. Follow any written safety signs or guidelines.

Photography Tips: The Provan Gas Works gives a unique setting for shooters, mixing industrial history with modern scenery.

Here are some tips to capture the spirit of this famous site: industrial shadows: contrast with nature; and historical context: include features that show the gas works' place in Glasgow's past, such as old train lines or surrounding buildings. Creative Angles: Look for odd angles and views to catch the gas tanks, such as reflections in puddles or through fences. With these tips, you're ready to discover and shoot the Provan Gas Works. Whether you're a history buff, an industrial building fan, or a shooter looking for a unique subject, this site offers a glimpse into Glasgow's famous past and its ongoing storyline.

Crookston Castle,

Crookston Castle, located south of the city center, is the only remaining medieval castle and the second oldest building in Glasgow, topped only by the 12th-century church. Built by the Stewarts of Danley around 1400 AD, its tall center tower and high setting offer sweeping views of the nearby area. It is thought that Mary, Queen of Scots, once lived in the palace, much of which was damaged and then rebuilt following a siege in 1544. During the Second World War, the edifice's strategic location led to its employment as a watch tower. As of today, the castle is owned and handled on behalf of tourists by the National Trust for Scotland.

How to get there: Crookston Castle, Glasgow's only remaining medieval castle, is a historical treasure waiting to be found. To visit this famous spot, set your plan for 170 Brockburn Road, Glasgow, G53 5RY1. If you're coming by train, the nearest stops are Bellgrove and Alexandra Parade. From there, a short bus ride will whisk you away to the castle's walls. For those who prefer to bike, the National Bike Network offers routes that pass near the castle, allowing for a beautiful trip through Glasgow's history.

The Best Time to Visit: The Castle welcomes tourists throughout the year, but the ideal time to step back into Scotland's ancient past is between April and September, from 9:30 a.m. up to 5:30 p.m., with the last entry at 5:00 p.m. These months offer longer days and better chances of clear weather, making them perfect for exploring the castle's nooks and crannies. Remember, the castle is closed on Thursdays and Fridays from October to March, so plan your visit accordingly.

Safety Tips: While Crookston Castle is a famous place, it's important to visit responsibly. Stick to the marked paths and obey any obstacles or signs. The castle's ruins can be uneven, so wear strong footwear. Keep children close, especially near the castle's higher points. If you're coming alone, let someone know your plans.

Photography Tips: Crookston Castle's old stones and sweeping views offer a feast for the eyes.

Here are some tips to catch its essence: Climb to the top: Ascend the castle for a stunning view of southeast Glasgow—a great background for your photos. Morning Light: Arrive early in the morning for soft, diffused lighting that will give your photos a magical quality.

Historical Context: Try to include aspects that tell a story, like the difference between the old stones and the current cities. Play with angles: Experiment with different angles to showcase the castle's unique design and its place in the environment. With these tips, you're ready to explore Crookston Castle. Whether you're a history lover, a photography aficionado, or simply want a link to Scotland's past, this castle offers a journey through time. So grab your camera, lace up your walking shoes, and immerse yourself in the history of the Stewarts of Darnley.

Seven Lochs Wetland Park.

Seven Lochs Wetland Park, spanning across 20 square kilometers of lakes, woods, and fields, is the largest wildlife park in Greater Glasgow and a vestige of the last Ice Age. Formerly home to an ample coal industry, this natural area plays host to a myriad of bird species, including buzzards, willow warblers, chiffchaffs, and whitethroats, among others. As its name suggests, the nature reserve is home to seven big lochs: Bishop Loch, Hogganfield Loch, Lochend Loch, Frankfield Loch, Woodend Loch, Garnqueen Loch, and Johnston Loch, but there are also several smaller ones in between.

As the park is crisscrossed by more than 50 kilometers of paths and bicycle tracks, it offers a much-needed break from the rush and bustle of the city. Aside from its natural worth, the place also has its fair share of historical importance; stone and flint tools dating back more than

10,000 years were found at Woodend Loch, suggesting that the area was home to some of Scotland's oldest people.

How to get there: Seven Lochs Wetland Park, a vast oasis of calm, sits between Glasgow's east end and Coatbridge

1. To engage yourself in this urban nature park, you can start your trip at one of the four tourist centers. Public transportation is easy, with several train stops nearby, including Stepps, Easterhouse, Gartcosh, and Robroyston

2. If you're driving, the park is easily approachable via the M8 and M80 freeways, with parking available at the tourist centers.

The Best Time to Visit: This green area is open year-round, but each season offers a unique charm. Spring and summer bring a chorus of bird songs and growing plants, making it an ideal time for nature enthusiasts. The park's hours are from 10:00 a.m. until 6:00 p.m., giving you plenty of sunshine to explore. For a peaceful experience, visit on weekdays when the paths are less crowded.

Safety Tips: While Seven Lochs Wetland Park is a safe and welcome place for tourists, it's always good to keep a few safety tips in mind: stay on marked trails and respect the native environment. Keep dogs on a leash to protect the wildlife. Bring water and food, especially if you plan to walk the longer trails. Be aware of the weather and dress appropriately.

Photography Tips: The park's various environments offer countless photography possibilities. Here are some tips to help you catch the beauty of Seven Lochs: Wildlife Wonders: Bring a zoom lens to capture the park's abundant birds without bothering them. Landscape Layers: Use the rule of thirds to arrange your shots, with lochs, forests, and skies creating layers of interest. Calm rivers provide perfect views of the sky and greenery, adding balance to your pictures.

Macro Magic: Don't ignore the small details; a macro lens can show the complex patterns of leaves, flowers, and animals. With these tips, you're ready to explore Seven Lochs Wetland Park. Whether you're wanting a peaceful escape or an adventure in the great outdoors, this park offers a bit of wilderness in the heart of the city. So pack your camera, lace up your walking boots, and set out to find the natural wonders that await.

Govanhill Baths

Govanhill Baths, Glasgow's only remaining Edwardian public baths, are the last of their kind in the city. Built-in 1917, the building represents the architectural style of that time, with features typical of public bathhouses in the early 20th century, such as big windows and unique, bright bricks. The site first opened its doors in the 1910s, and despite a period of shutdown in 2001, the building is now under repair following a long community effort to ensure its survival.

The renovation plans, under the guidance of the Govanhill Baths Community Trust, include three fully working swimming pools as well as an art workshop, kitchen, and gym, all of which are open to members of the public and the local community. Seasonal events, including Christmas markets and an international fair, also take place in this famous building.

Getting There: Navigating to Govanhill Baths Govanhill Baths is located at 99 Calder Street, Govanhill, Glasgow, Scotland. If you're planning a visit, the easiest way to get there is by public transport or car. For those using public transport, buses and trains run daily to the area, with stops within walking distance of the baths. If you're driving, you'll find on-street parking available, but do be aware of the local parking laws. When to Experience Govanhill Baths:

The Best Time to Visit While the exact opening hours can change, Govanhill Baths is usually open from Monday to Friday at 10:00 a.m. to 4:00 p.m. The best time to visit would be during the weekdays to avoid possible weekend crowds. Keep an eye on their official website or local news for any special events or programs that might be happening, which could provide a unique visiting experience.

Safety Tips: Ensuring a Secure Visit When visiting Govanhill Baths, like any public place, it's important to stay aware of your surroundings. Here are a few safety tips: Keep your things close and safe. Follow any written safety instructions, especially if you plan to swim. Be respectful of the area and other guests, as Govanhill Baths is a community-focused site.

Photography Tips: Capturing Govanhill Baths Govanhill Baths, with its Edwardian design and community spirit, offers a wealth of picture possibilities. Here are some tips to help you catch its essence: Use natural light to your advantage, especially in the early morning or late afternoon.

Focus on the building's features and the balance of light and dark. Respect the privacy of others; always ask for permission before taking photos of people. Share your pictures with the community; it's a great way to meet and add to the story of Govanhill Baths. In closing, Govanhill Baths is more than just a building; it's a testament to the resilience and spirit of the Govanhill community.

Whether you're a local or a tourist, there's something for everyone to discover and enjoy. So, pack your camera, enjoy the community vibe, and get ready for an enriching experience at Govanhill Baths. Safe travels and happy snaps!

Pollok Beech Pollok House

The Pollok Beech Pollok House, the alleged creation of Scottish builder William Adam, is an opulent Georgian-style home on the outskirts of Glasgow, dating back to the mid-18th century. The land formerly belonged to the powerful Stirling-Maxwell family, who lived on this spot for 600 years and 27 generations. One member of the family, Sir John Stirling-Maxwell, was the Conservative MP for Glasgow from 1895 to 1906. He died at Pollok House in 1956.

Although the house itself is closed for refurbishment until 2025, guests can still enjoy the nearby grounds and gardens, including the Woodland Garden, home to the Pollok Beech. This 250-year-old wizened tree was recognized in 2002 as one of the top hundred heritage trees in Scotland. The oddly shaped beech grows on a mound that scholars believe marks the site of an ancient castle, possibly from the 13th century.

How to get there: Nestled within the calm stretch of Pollok Country Park, finding the Pollok Beech is a trip through Glasgow's green history. For those who rely on public transport, buses marked 57/57A, 3, and 34/34A will take you straight to the park from Glasgow city center. If you prefer the train, alight at Pollokshaws West station; from there, a short walk across the bridge and to the left on Pollokshaws Road gets you to the park entrance.

The Best Time to Visit: Pollok Country Park, home of the Pollok Beech, is open 24/7, all year round. The best time to visit is probably during the spring and summer months, when the scenery is lush and the gardens are in full bloom. However, the park's beauty is not lost in the fall, with the beech's leaves turning a red hue, or even in the winter, when the stark trees against a gray sky create a dramatic scene.

Safety Tips: While the park offers a quiet escape, it's important to stay aware of your surroundings. Stick to the marked paths, especially when going near the Pollok Beech, as its age means it could be fragile in some places. Ensure you're prepared for Scotland's changeable weather by dressing in layers and bringing wet gear. Lastly, know that the park's car parks charge at 10 a.m. to 6 p.m., so have some change ready if you're driving.

Photography Tips: The Pollok Beech, with its unique shape and storied past, is a photographer's joy. Here are some tips to catch its essence: lighting: visit during the golden hours, soon after sunrise or before sunset, to take advantage of the soft, diffused light. Composition: To frame the beech, use the rule of thirds, putting it off-center for a more exciting picture.

Focus: Highlight the textures of the beech's base and branches by using a small depth of field. Storytelling: Include elements like the surrounding woods or the nearby Pollok House to add meaning to the beech's long past. In catching the Pollok Beech, you're not just taking a picture; you're saving a piece of Glasgow's soul. Whether you're a local or a tourist, this big beech is a sign of the city's ongoing link to nature and the past. So, grab your camera and let Pollok Beech's story play through your lens.

Hope Sculpture:

As home to the 2021 COP26 climate meeting, Glasgow was awarded the Hope Sculpture, a donation from more than 50 companies to the city to mark this important event. Materials for the sculpture were given free of charge, and the artwork was made by artist Steuart Padwick. The sculpture, showing an age-, gender-, and race-neutral kid with spread arms atop a tower, is famous for several reasons. It is the first sculpture in the UK to be built from 100% cement-free concrete, with a carbon footprint roughly 70% lower than standard concrete.

Continuing the environmental theme, the art makes use of salvaged elements, including gas pipes. Freely available to the public, this artwork is situated in the Cuningar Loop, a forest park built in 2010 in a bend of the River Clyde. As well as having the Hope Sculpture, the park features several riverside walks and bicycle paths, Scotland's first outdoor climbing park, and the Cuningar Stones, an art project by Glasgow artist James Winnett that charts the local history of the area across 15 fixed stones.

How to get there: The Hope Sculpture is situated at 810 7th Ave., between 53rd St. and 52nd St., New York, NY 100192. To visit, you can easily walk from the 7th Ave. train station, which is just a minute away, or from the 50th St. station, a mere three-minute walk. The sculpture's central position in Midtown makes it approachable from different parts of the city.

The Best Time to Visit: While the sculpture can be viewed at any time, the best experience is during daylight hours, when the details and the spirit of the sculpture can be fully enjoyed. The area is famous and busy, mirroring the non-stop energy of New York, so an afternoon visit means you can see the sculpture in its urban context.

Safety Tips: When visiting Sculpture, it's important to be aware of the busy Midtown traffic. Always cross streets at marked crosswalks and follow traffic signs. Keep your things safe, as busy areas can attract pickpockets. Lastly, be aware of the weather conditions and dress properly to enjoy your visit comfortably. Photography Tips:

Photographing the Hope Sculpture offers a chance to catch the soul of New York's spirit. Here are some tips to help you get the best shots: lighting: aim for the golden hours to capture the sculpture's warm glow from sunrise or sunset.

Perspective: Experiment with different angles to determine which view of the work is most appealing. A low position can make it look more menacing.

Details: While removing the background, use a small depth of field to focus on the sculpture's detailed details. Storytelling: Try to include parts of the local cityscape to give meaning to the Hope Sculpture's place in the heart of New York. In shooting the Hope Sculpture, you're catching a piece of art that stands for hope and progress.

Whether you're a seasoned shooter or just snapping pictures with your phone, the sculpture offers a unique chance to reflect on the city's dynamic character and your hopes for the future.

Lesser-Known Historical Sites:

Glasgow, rich in history and culture, harbors several lesser-known historical gems that offer a more personal glimpse into the city's past.

These places provide a great option for those looking to explore beyond the usual tourist spots.

Glasgow Necropolis. situated on a hill facing Glasgow Cathedral, Glasgow Necropolis is a vast Victorian garden cemetery full of history, art, and architectural wonder. Known as the city of the dead, this spot offers a peaceful yet emotional study of Glasgow's past.

The Best Time to Visit: Visiting early in the morning or late in the afternoon offers the best lighting for photos and a more private experience. These times allow you to enjoy the quiet atmosphere and detailed details of the landmarks without the influence of strong noon light or larger groups.

Safety Tips: While walking through the Necropolis, it's important to stay on the main routes. The ground can be uneven, with old concrete paths and occasional steep inclines, making it easy to trip if one is not careful. Suitable boots and careful steps are recommended.

Photography Tips: The Necropolis is a haven for shooters, especially those interested in historical and building topics capture the essence of this spot, focus on the Victorian-era landmarks in the setting of Glasgow city at sunset. This time of day provides dramatic lighting and enhances the eerie beauty of the graveyard. Experimenting with different angles can also give fascinating shadows and highlight the detailed craftsman.

Provand's Lordship: located in the heart of Glasgow, is the oldest house in the city, providing an interesting glimpse into medieval Scotland. Built in 1471, it originally served as part of St. Nicholas's Hospital and has since become a beloved historical museum, attracting tourists with its well-preserved architecture and fascinating past.

The Best Time to Visit: Visiting in the summer is particularly satisfying, as the medical herb garden, a replica of a 15th-century garden, is in full this colorful show not only improves Provand's Lordship's aesthetic appeal but also offers a physical journey through the uses of different plants during medieval times.

Safety Tips: While the area around Provand's Lordship is usually safe, tourists should stick to typical city measures. Keep personal items safe and stay aware of your surroundings, especially during busy times when the small passageways inside can become quite crowded.

Photography Tips: For picture lovers, the interior of Provand's Lordship presents a unique opportunity. The historical furniture and the dramatic lighting inside make a perfect setting for detail shots. Capturing the detailed woodwork and period items allows photographers to express the rich historical spirit of the house.

Experience and Engagement: Each room inside Provand's Lordship tells a different story, filled with period furniture and historical items that show the lifestyle of its previous inmates. The house also features educational signs and engaging displays that improve the tourist experience, making it not just a walk but a step back in time. The best time to visit: For a truly immersing experience, timing your visit to meet with a live show is key.

Panopticon: The Panopticon hosts a range of shows that echo the past, from traditional music hall acts to silent films and more modern performances. These events not only provide fun but also improve your understanding of the venue's historical worth.

Safety Tips: Situated in Glasgow's busy city center, the Panopticon is in a lively area visited by both locals and tourists. While usually safe, tourists should remain cautious about personal items and stay aware of their surroundings, especially during evening events.

Photography Tips: Capturing the interior of the Britannia Panopticon during a show offers a rare chance to picture a piece of history in motion. The elaborate details and the warm glow of the stage lights create a compelling atmosphere. For the best shots, focus on the contact between artists and the historic settings, which highlights the music hall's preserved architectural features.

The best times to visit: The Hidden Gardens are during the spring and fall months. In spring, the grounds are alive with the bright colors of blooming flowers, creating a beautiful setting that feels almost magical. Autumn brings a palette of bright reds and golds, along with falling leaves that carpet the paths and add crunchy music to your stroll.

Hidden Gardens

Safety Tips: The Hidden Gardens are known for their calm and friendly atmosphere, making them a safe location for people and families alike. Visitors are urged to relax and enjoy the calm of the grounds. However, as with any public place, keeping personal items safe and staying aware of your surroundings is always recommended.

Photographers will find The Hidden Gardens a satisfying subject, particularly due to the mix of natural light and the garden's modern sculptures. Early mornings or late afternoons offer the best light for shooting, leaving soft glows and dramatic shadows. Focusing on how light interacts with the sculptures and plants can give amazing visual tales that capture the spirit of this secret gem.

Each of these places offers unique views into Glasgow's diverse history and culture, providing a quiet break from the busy city life. Respect the places, keep safety in mind, and take plenty of photos to remember your stay.

Unique Glasgow Experiences:

Whether you are a history fan eager to trace the steps of the past, an art lover wanting to engage in a mix of classical and modern expressions, or a culinary explorer ready to taste new dishes based on Scottish tradition, Glasgow promises an array of unforgettable moments. This guide aims to reveal some of the most distinctive activities and sights that set Glasgow as a top location for those looking to experience something truly exceptional.

1. Discover the hidden gems of Glasgow's architecture. Glasgow's architectural landscape is a visual delight, showing a peaceful mix of Victorian grandeur, Edwardian elegance, and bold modernist designs. Begin your architecture tour at the famous Glasgow School of Art, a gem created by the legendary Charles Rennie Mackintosh. Despite suffering from fire damage, the ongoing repair efforts offer an interesting glimpse into Mackintosh's innovative vision. Venture beyond the well-trodden road to discover Mackintosh's lesser-known works, such as The Lighthouse, his debut public commission, which now houses Scotland's Centre for Design and Architecture.

2. Dive into Glasgow's Vibrant Music Scene. Glasgow's title as a UNESCO City of Music is well-deserved, thanks to its varied music scene that crosses diverse styles and epochs. Experience the city's

musical heartbeat at King Tut's Wah Wah Hut, a place known for finding bands like Oasis. The club hosts a varied cast, with both rising local stars and known acts. For those drawn towards traditional sounds, an evening at The Ben Nevis offers a private setting to enjoy true Scottish folk music, linking with Glasgow's rich musical history.

3. Savor the local flavors. Glasgow's culinary scene is as diverse as it is innovative, making it a critical stop for anyone looking to experience Scottish food with a modern twist. The Ubiquitous Chip, located in the beautiful Ashton Lane, offers a creative menu that reimagines traditional Scottish ingredients in a modern cooking context. For vegans, Mono provides a friendly setting with its range of vegan meals, including a unique take on traditional haggis, followed by an array of locally made beers.

4. Engage with Glasgow's rich artistic heritage. The Kelvingrove Art Gallery and Museum stands as a symbol of Glasgow's artistic history, with works that run from the Renaissance to the Scottish Colourists. The Gallery of Modern Art is an exciting place for contemporary art fans, offering cutting-edge shows in the heart of Royal Exchange Square. The city's Mural Trail adds a modern twist to Glasgow's art scene, changing everyday buildings into a lively show of street art from local and foreign artists.

5. Experience Glasgow's Green Spaces. Known kindly as the "Dear Green Place," Glasgow is rich in vast parks and lush gardens, giving more green areas per head than any other city in the UK. The Botanic Gardens provide a quiet escape with their vast plant collections and the historic Kibble Palace glasshouse. For those wanting a more extensive getaway, Pollok Country Park, with its wide forests and the famous Burrell Collection, offers a perfect mix of nature and culture.

6. Explore Glasgow's nautical heritage at the Riverside Museum, built by the famous architect Zaha Hadid, where tourists can dig into Glasgow's famed shipbuilding past. The museum's collection includes everything from old cars to trains to ships, capturing the city's economic history. A visit to the Tall Ship, docked outside the museum, offers a physical link to Glasgow's nautical past, allowing tourists to experience life aboard a traditional ship.

In sum, Glasgow is a city that offers a wealth of unique and memorable experiences, showing its rich cultural history and dynamic modern vibe. Glasgow invites you to explore its many wonders, from its magnificent buildings and lively music scene to its diverse food choices and bright green spaces. So, bring your sense of adventure and prepare to discover the heart and soul of Scotland's most lively city.

Sustainable Travel in Glasgow:

As more tourists become aware of their environmental effects, towns like Glasgow are stepping up as prime locations for sustainable tourism. Known for its rich history and dedication to green efforts, Glasgow offers a variety of ways to enjoy its charms safely.

Utilize Glasgow's comprehensive public transport. One of Glasgow's cleanest features is its highly efficient public transportation system, which serves as a backbone for sustainable travel within the city. By depending on this network of buses, subways, and trains, tourists can greatly lower their carbon footprint while experiencing the city genuinely. The Glasgow Subway, a historic and efficient subway, rounds the city center and provides a quick and eco-friendly way to hop between major sights. For locations outside the train line, the vast bus system serves nearly every part of the city and beyond. For tourists, buying a day or multi-day pass can ease travel and support the use of public transport over car rentals.

Explore by bike. Cycling is another great way to explore Glasgow sustainably. The city supports a healthy riding infrastructure, including specific bike lanes and paths that ensure safety and accessibility. Glasgow's Nextbike program, a public bike-sharing service, is great for short trips around the city or relaxing walks through its beautiful roads.

Cycling not only allows you to reduce environmental impact but also provides the freedom to explore areas less available by public transport, such as the beautiful Clyde River route or the artistic hubs in Glasgow's West End. Support eco-friendly local businesses. Glasgow's drive for sustainability is also evident in its growing community of eco-conscious businesses.

By choosing to eat at places like Locavore, which gets organic food from local farms, or shopping at zero-waste shops, guests can enjoy Glasgow's local tastes and goods without the worry of environmental harm. These businesses often go beyond lowering carbon emissions by acting in ways that promote wildlife, reduce trash, and support local economies.

Enjoy Glasgow's lush green spaces. The city's numerous parks and grounds offer ample chances for healthy tourist activities. The Glasgow Botanic Gardens are not only a place for rest and pleasure, but they also contribute to protection efforts by housing plant species from around the world.

Pollok Country Park, another important green area, offers a chance to explore old forests and is home to the famous Burrell Collection, showing the city's historical and cultural items. Activities like guided nature walks or wildlife spotting in these parks can help you better understand Scotland's natural history and the importance of protecting it.

Choose sustainable accommodations. When it comes to housing, Glasgow offers different safe choices. Eco-friendly hotels in Glasgow are pioneering in terms of lowering water usage, adopting energy-efficient systems, and using sustainable materials in their operations. These hotels are recognized by organizations like Green Tourism, giving you confidence that your stay is backed by environmentally responsible practices. Staying at these places not only reduces your trip's effect but also helps the greater green goals of the city's tourist sector.

Participate in eco-friendly events. Glasgow is home to numerous fairs and events year-round, many of which are green. For instance, the Glasgow Film Festival uses eco-friendly practices by reducing trash, supporting digital tickets, and encouraging guests to use public transport. Participating in these events allows visitors to interact with local culture and community while supporting efforts to host sustainable gatherings.

Make a positive impact. Traveling wisely in Glasgow provides a rich and satisfying experience that aligns with the global shift towards more responsible tourism. By choosing eco-friendly transport, supporting local businesses, enjoying nature places, picking green lodgings, and attending sustainable events, you contribute to the protection and improvement of Glasgow's environmental and cultural setting. As you explore Glasgow, your choices help ensure that the city stays lively and healthy for future tourists and locals alike.

Bonus: Insider Tips from Locals

Bonus 1:

L **ocal Customs and Etiquette:**
When visiting Glasgow, knowing the local traditions and politeness can greatly improve your experience and help you fit in with the residents. Glasgow, known for its friendly and lively atmosphere, is a city where cultural details and social etiquette are understood and observed. This guide will provide you with insights into the local practices and etiquette that define the everyday lives of Glaswegians, ensuring a smooth and enjoyable visit.

Greetings and social interactions in Glasgow, as in much of Scotland, a friendly attitude is highly valued. When meeting someone for the first time, a handshake is usual, followed by a smile and direct eye contact. It's usual to use titles and nicknames until asked to use first names, although Glaswegians are quickly relaxed and warm in their interactions.

Once you become familiar, don't be surprised by the frequent use of terms of endearment like "dear," "hen," or "love," which are signs of friendship. Conversations often start with the weather, which can be a safe subject due to Glasgow's typically changeable environment. Feel free to join in with light-hearted comments about the rain or the cold; it's a shared experience that can be a conversation starter! Pubs and social pubs play a key role in social life in Glasgow.

When joining a group at a bar, it's standard practice to take turns buying a 'round' of drinks for the whole table. This is not just a nice act, but a deeply ingrained part of our society. If someone gives you a drink, you are usually expected to return the favor later in the session. When in bars, also be aware of the local sports culture, especially football. Glasgow is home to two big football teams—Rangers and Celtic—and it's recommended to avoid wearing team colors unless you are sure of the company and setting, as this can be a sensitive subject.

Dining Etiquette: When eating out, especially in nicer places, it is normal to wait to be served. In Glasgow, table manners are traditional: keep your hands visible, shoulders off the table, and try to eat quietly. Tipping is usual in Glasgow as in the rest of the UK, and leaving 10-15% of the bill at restaurants is normal practice if service charges are not included.

Understanding the queue is a serious business in Glasgow. Whether it's waiting for a bus, at the store checkout, or getting tickets, jumping the queue is considered very rude. Always take your place at the end of the line and wait for your turn. This respect for order is seen as a sign of care for others.

Dress Code Glaswegians are quite stylish but useful, given the often chilly and wet weather. When packing for Glasgow, include layers that you can add or remove as needed. If you're visiting bars or going out to dinner, smart casual wear is usually okay. For theater, music, or more expensive places, a more dressy outfit may be acceptable.

Respect for privacy and personal space: while Glaswegians are known for their warmth and kindness, they also value private and personal space. It's important not to be too nosy with personal questions, especially upon first meeting. When talking, keeping a proper space is respected unless the other person signals otherwise.

By following these rules on local customs and etiquette, you'll not only show respect for the local culture but also improve your own experience in Glasgow. The city's friendly nature and lively community life are best enjoyed when you connect with the locals in a way that is polite and thoughtful.

Whether you're exploring the historical sights, enjoying a meal, or having a night out at the pub, knowing and accepting these local customs will help you feel like a part of Glasgow's lively culture.

Bonus 2:

Shopping Guide:

Glasgow, with its rich cultural mix and lively creative scene, offers a wealth of buying choices that run from high-end shops to odd local markets. For guests looking to take home a piece of this lively city, this guide shows the top spots to shop for gifts and local goods. Whether you're looking for traditional Scottish things, modern art, or unique

BONUS: INSIDER TIPS FROM LOCALS

goods, Glasgow's various shopping places provide something for every taste.

1. Buchanan Street and the Style Mile Start your shopping journey on Buchanan Street, part of Glasgow's famous "Style Mile." This busy public road is lined with a mix of high-street shops, fashion boutiques, and department stores such as House of Fraser, which offers a range of luxury brands under one roof. For uniquely Scottish things, don't miss the Buchanan Galleries, where you can find shops selling traditional Scottish.

2. Barras Market, located in Glasgow's East End. This weekend market is a great trove of antiques, retro clothes, vinyl records, and handmade goods. It's also a fantastic place to pick up unique Glasgow gifts, from homemade jewelry to craft food products, all while taking in the lively atmosphere that reflects Glasgow's true spirit.

3. The Hidden Lane: Tucked away in the Finnieston area, The Hidden Lane is a lively community of artists' workshops, stores, and bars. This off-the-beaten-path gem is great for those looking to buy one-of-a-kind art pieces, handmade crafts, or unique jewelry straight from local artists. Visiting The Hidden Lane not only allows you to find unique gifts but also gives you the chance to meet the makers and learn about their craft.

4. Ashton Lane, a beautiful cobbled backstreet in the West End, is famous for its lively nightlife and Victorian architecture. However, it's also home to cozy stores and independent shops. Here, you can find everything from Scottish-made pictures and books to custom clothes and specialty foods. The lane is especially charming in the evening, with its fairy lights and busy bistros, making it a perfect spot for a relaxed shopping experience.

5. Princes Square, located on Buchanan Street, is a beautifully rebuilt 19th-century building turned shopping and eating center. It houses an odd mix of brand stores, craft shops, and expensive places. For exclusive Scottish designer clothes and expensive items, this is the place to go. The beautiful interior, complete with wrought iron work and a glass roof, adds to the overall shopping experience.

6. Argyll Arcade If you're in the market for jewelry, the Argyll Arcade, one of Europe's oldest covered shopping arcades, is a must-visit. This historic alley boasts over 30 jewelers and diamond merchants, offering everything from custom pieces to old gems. It's an ideal place to find a special piece of jewelry to remember your trip.

7. Glasgow's West End For a varied shopping experience, discover Glasgow's West End. This artsy area is filled with secondhand shops, bookstores, and ethnic markets. The Great Western Road and Byres Road are particularly good for browsing a wide array of stores that sell everything from retro fashion and second-hand books to foreign spices and homemade soaps.

Shopper'saradise Glasgow offers an exciting and varied shopping scene that caters to all tastes and budgets. From busy markets and quaint streets to luxury shops and historic alleys, the city is a shopper's dream, rich with chances to find both traditional Scottish gifts and modern goods. Remember, each purchase not only serves as a memory of your trips but also helps the local economy, making your shopping experience both satisfying and effective.

Bonus 3:

Tips for Traveling with Kids:

Glasgow is a great location for families, with a wide range of activities that cater to children of all ages. From engaging museums and expansive parks to kid-friendly eating and educational experiences, the city is packed with options to keep your little ones engaged and entertained. This guide offers useful tips and advice for parents going with children to Glasgow, ensuring a smooth and fun trip for the whole family.

1. Choosing the Right Accommodation When traveling with kids, the choice of lodging can make a significant difference in your trip's success. Look for family-friendly hotels or leased apartments in central locations such as the City Center or West End. These places are not only safe but also close to many of the main sites, reducing travel time and making it easier to return to your room for breaks or naps. Many hotels offer family rooms or linked rooms with features such as cribs and high chairs, which can be very helpful when traveling with young children.

2. Engaging activities for all ages: Glasgow is filled with activities that are both fun and educational for kids. The Riverside Museum, for example, is a transport museum with engaging exhibits and a vast collection of vehicles, from old steam trains to modern electric cars, that can interest children and adults alike.

Another must-visit is the Glasgow Science Centre, which features hands-on science exhibits, a theater, and live science shows meant to excite young minds. For a more relaxing day out, head to one of Glasgow's many parks. PoPollok Country Park is a great choice, offering wide open spaces for children to play, as well as a chance to see Highland cattle and visit the award-winning Burrell Collection. Glasgow Green, the city's largest park, has a big playground and is often the site for family-friendly events and fairs.

3. Family-friendly dining in Glasgow boasts a variety of eating choices that are great for families. Many places offer children's meals and are provided with high chairs and coloring books to keep kids occupied. For a unique experience, visit the Willow Tea Rooms, which not only offers kid-friendly food but also gives you a taste of Glasgow's rich past in a building built by Charles Rennie Mackintosh.

Cafes and bistros, such as those in the West End, often have a relaxed setting that can be more comfortable for families with young children. Look for places that source local products, so you can introduce your kids to Scottish cooking in a fun and healthy way.

4. Navigating a city with children requires some planning. Practical Tips for City Navigation Glasgow's public transport system, including buses and trains, provides an easy way to get around. Consider getting a family day pass, which can be cost-effective and remove the hassle of buying passes for each trip. When exploring the city, it's a good idea to have a lightweight stroller for younger children. Many of Glasgow's streets are pedestrian-friendly, especially around big shopping places like Buchanan Street; however, dress in waterproof coats and umbrellas to prepare for the occasional rain.

Safety and emergency services: Knowing ahead of time where to find medical help can ease your mind when traveling with kids. Glasgow has several hospitals with emergency services, and shops are readily available throughout the city for any minor illnesses or medical needs.

It's also smart to have a list of emergency contacts, including the local emergency number, which is 999 in the UK.

Having fun in Glasgow with the kids: Traveling with children in Glasgow can be a lovely experience. With the right planning and understanding of what the city has to offer, you can make memorable moments for your family. Whether visiting Glasgow's museums, enjoying its beautiful parks, or trying its kid-friendly places, you'll find that the city's welcoming atmosphere makes it an ideal destination for family visitors.

Bonus 4:

How to Make Your Trip Unforgettable:

Glasgow, Scotland's lively cultural hub, offers a rich mix of experiences that can make any visit memorable. From its ancient buildings and busy arts scene to its friendly locals and green places, Glasgow has a charm all its own. Whether you're a first-time visitor or returning to explore the city, these tips will help you make the most of your trip and leave with memorable memories.

1. Dive deep into Glasgow's cultural scene. To truly experience Glasgow, engage yourself in the culture it offers. Begin with a visit to the famous Glasgow School of Art, built by Charles Rennie Mackintosh, where you can take a guided tour to understand its architectural importance and artistic impact. Explore the city's rich music scene by watching a live band at King Tut's Wah Wah Hut, a place famous for starting the careers of Oasis and other notable bands.

2. Art fans should not miss the Kelvingrove Art Gallery and Museum, home to a vast collection that runs from guns and armor to a Salvador Dali work. The nearby Riverside Museum, with its fascinating exhibits on transportation and travel, as well as the stunning Zaha Hadid-designed building, is another must-visit for those interested in modern design and marine history.

Engage with the locals. Glaswegians are known for their kindness and generosity. Engaging with locals can improve your trip experience, giving you insights into the city's culture and secret gems that you might not find in guidebooks. Spend some time in a traditional bar, where you can strike up a chat over a pint of local ale or whisky. VisitVisit local markets, such as the Barras Market, to meet with sellers and artists and perhaps pick up unique gifts.

3. Experience the festivals. Glasgow's calendar is packed with events that showcase its artistic range and cultural vibrancy. Plan your starnear events, such as the Glasgow International Comedy Festival, the Celtic Connections music festival, or the West End Festival. These events offer chances to experience the city at its most lively, with live shows, parades, and community activities that bring together locals and tourists.

4. Take a Culinary Journey: Glasgow's food scene is a mirror of its diverse and international spirit. Don't leave without trying traditional Scottish foods like haggis, neeps, and tatties or delighting in a filling, full Scottish breakfast. For a modern spin on local food, eat at places that highlight sustainable Scottish products, such as The Gannet or Ubiquitous Chip. Also, discover the growing veggie and vegetarian scene in places like Finnieston.

5. Explore the outdoors. Despite being a busy city, Glasgow offers

numerous green havens. Take a relaxing walk through the Botanic Gardens or spend an afternoon at Pollok Country Park, where you can visit the Burrell Collection and even see Highland cattle. For a more active day, take a bike and ride along the River Clyde, enjoying the cityscapes and stopping at Glasgow Green for lunch.

6. Capture memories. Last but not least, make sure to record your trip. Take photos and videos of your adventures, from the amazing views atop the Lighthouse viewing platform to the busy streets of the Merchant City. Keep a trip diary to note down details of your adventures, the people you meet, and how each experience made you feel. Every trip to Glasgow is unique, and the city offers countless ways to make your visit special.

By planning and enjoying all that Glasgow has to offer, from its historic sites and cultural events to its culinary treats and friendly pubs, you can ensure your journey is not just memorable but truly unique. Remember, the best trip experiences come from exploring with an open heart and a curious mind.

Printed in Great Britain
by Amazon